COMMUNITY COHESION AND HOUSING: A GOOD PRACTICE GUIDE

JOHN PERRY AND BOB BLACKABY

PUBLISHED BY THE
CHARTERED INSTITUTE OF HOUSING
AND THE HOUSING CORPORATION

The Chartered Institute of Housing

The Chartered Institute of Housing is the professional organisation for people who work in housing. Its purpose is to maximise the contribution housing professionals make to the wellbeing of communities. The Chartered Institute has over 20,000 members across the UK and the Asian Pacific working in a range of organisations – including housing associations, local authorities, arms length management organisations, the private sector and educational institutions.

Chartered Institute of Housing
Octavia House, Westwood Way
Coventry CV4 8JP
Telephone: 024 7685 1700
www.cih.org

The Housing Corporation

The Housing Corporation is the government agency which registers, regulates and funds over 1,500 social landlords in England which between them provide 2 million homes. The Corporation has an important role as a promoter of good practice in the social housing sector.

The Housing Corporation
149 Tottenham Court Road
London W1T 7BN
Telephone: 020 7393 2000
www.housingcorp.gov.uk

Community Cohesion and Housing: a good practice guide
Written by John Perry and Bob Blackaby

© Chartered Institute of Housing and the Housing Corporation 2007
ISBN 978 1 905018 61 1

Graphic design by Jeremy Spencer
Cover photograph by Daniela Andreea Spyropoulos/istockphoto.com
Printed by Genesis Print and Marketing

Contents

Acknowledgements

The Chartered Institute of Housing would like to thank the Housing Corporation for providing funding for the publication of this guide and for the support of Steve Douglas, its Acting Chief Executive (who was also a member of the Commission on Integration and Cohesion).

Grateful thanks are also due to the members of the reading panel who provided helpful suggestions and commented on draft material:

Jane Allanson	Chartered Institute of Housing
Jas Bains	Ashram Housing Association
Harris Beider	Consultant
Ted Cantle	Institute for Community Cohesion and IDeA
David Carrigan	Housing Corporation
Ruby Dixon	IDeA
Joanna Dooher	Audit Commission
Pat Hobbs	Leicester City Council
Atul Patel	LHA-ASRA
David Robinson	Sheffield Hallam University
Anil Singh	Manningham Housing Association
Sally Thomas	Social Regeneration Consultants

Bob Blackaby was the author of the original, 2004 edition of the guide. Many sections of his text have been incorporated in or adapted for the new version and he made a significant contribution to the new edition.

David Anderson and Ruby Dixon, who worked with the Commission on Integration and Cohesion, provided help with practical examples.

CIH is indebted to the many local authorities, housing associations and other organisations that provided details of their initiatives and programmes either directly or through the work of the Commission, or commented on elements of the guide.

John Perry
October, 2007

Glossary of acronyms used in the text

ALMO	arms length management organisation
ASB	anti-social behaviour
BME	black and minority ethnic
BVPI	best value performance indicator
CAA	Comprehensive Area Assessment
CBL	choice-based lettings
CDRP	Crime and Disorder Reduction Partnership
CEHR	Commission for Equality and Human Rights
CIH	Chartered Institute of Housing
CLG	Communities and Local Government (Department for)
CPA	Comprehensive Performance Assessment
CRE	Commission for Racial Equality
ESOL	English for speakers of other languages
GIS	geographical information systems
GO	Government Office
HA	housing association
hact	Housing Associations Charitable Trust
HCA	Housing Corporation Assessment
HMO	house in multiple occupation
HMR	housing market renewal
ICoCo	Institute for Community Cohesion
IDeA	Improvement and Development Agency for Local Government
JRF	Joseph Rowntree Foundation
KLOE	key line of enquiry
LA	local authority
LAA	Local Area Agreement
LB	London Borough
LGA	Local Government Association
LSP	Local Strategic Partnership
LSVT	large scale voluntary transfer
MBC	Metropolitan Borough Council
MRCO	migrant or refugee community organisation
PI	performance indicator
PCT	primary care trust
PSA	Public Service Agreement

CHAPTER 1

INTRODUCTION

What is the purpose of the guide?

A cohesive community is one that is in a state of wellbeing, harmony and stability. Policy and practice about community cohesion are about how everyone involved in a community can work together to create such cohesion. This guide aims to help housing organisations, housing professionals and the residents they work with to carry out this task.

One reason for having a guide is that concerns about cohesion breaking down have occurred for several reasons in the last few years – the disturbances that shook several northern towns in the summer of 2001, the London bombings in July 2005 and recent controversy about levels of migration. These events have prompted a series of formal inquiries. One of the main ones was led by Ted Cantle, was published in December 2001 and resulted in 'community cohesion' being defined and policy developed.

Then in 2006, concern about continuing problems, and the need to take a fresh look at the issues, led to the appointment of a new commission chaired by Darra Singh. The Commission's report, *Our Shared Future*, published in June, 2007, is set to have a considerable influence on government and local policy (details of the Commission's publications are at the end of this chapter).

In response to the Cantle report and subsequent policy guidance, the Chartered Institute of Housing and the Housing Corporation published, in 2004, the first edition of *Community Cohesion and Housing – A good practice guide*, written by Bob Blackaby. But as the Singh Commission's work was under way in 2007, CIH and the Housing Corporation agreed to produce this new edition, to reflect the Commission's recommendations and to update the advice to housing professionals, on the basis of the practical experience which has been developed in many places and in many housing organisations over the last three years.

Why a new guide?

The particular emphasis of the Singh Commission is on 'how local areas themselves can play a role in forging cohesive and resilient communities'. It challenges locally-based bodies such as local authorities and housing associations, and communities themselves, to take action at neighbourhood level – not waiting for policy to be determined nationally but taking the steps that seem right locally. This guide follows in the spirit of that approach, and is packed with practical examples of where this is already happening.

Another of the Commission's main messages is that society is changing rapidly, sometimes in areas of the country which have not previously experienced much change. Migrants now come to Britain from all over the world, not just places with traditional links to Britain. Some places are now experiencing what the Commission calls 'super-diversity' and guidance to practitioners must change accordingly.

While the Commission's report covered housing, this was not its main theme. Another purpose of this guide is therefore to fill out the ideas and proposals that the Commission made, take account of other studies related to housing, and provide a practical toolkit aimed specifically at housing providers and the residents with whom they work.

In doing so we have used not only the examples mentioned by the Commission but others that it did not publicise, or that have been gathered by CIH itself in the course of this work. We have used the experience of CIH in recent projects dealing with refugees and with new migrants from Eastern Europe, and used similar sources of examples from the Audit Commission and the IDeA. And we have talked to people on the ground who have experience of the issues, and who have been able to help in developing widely-applicable guidance.

Who is the guide for?

It is hoped that this guide will enable those working for housing organisations to see that they can make a positive contribution to the creation of more cohesive neighbourhoods. The guide should be of use to a variety of organisations involved in housing – to local authorities in their strategic and enabling role, to social landlords (local authorities, arms length management organisations and housing associations), to private developers and to those involved in 'housing exchange', particularly estate and lettings agents. It should be useful as well to people living in neighbourhoods, perhaps active as members of residents' groups, who are interested in creating more cohesive communities.

The guide should also be of value to government, regulatory and inspection bodies in helping them to develop appropriate guidance to housing organisations.

The guide assumes that readers are interested not just in 'housing' issues but in the wider neighbourhood dimensions of cohesion – which of course is essential if local approaches are actually to work. Most of the practical examples reflect this theme.

Because the terminology and recent policy initiatives have come from experience in England, the guide is oriented towards English organisations. However, it makes use of practical examples from Scotland and Wales, and it is hoped that the principles and experience it describes will also be useful to practitioners north and west of the borders. The guide does not, however, attempt to deal with the specific circumstances of Northern Ireland.

Readers should bear in mind that this is a policy area in which changes frequently occur. Details in the guide may therefore become out-of-date. However, the principles and practical advice are intended to be longer-lasting.

How was the guide compiled?

The starting point for the main text of the guide was the previous edition, but with considerable amendment and extra material drawn from recent policy and practical examples, especially relating to the Commission's work.

Over 60 practical examples have been included to show how housing and other organisations have tackled community cohesion in different parts of the UK. These have largely been drawn from the official sources mentioned above or from material available to CIH through its wider professional practice work.

Many of the examples are recently-started projects where it is too soon to evaluate the results. But they have all been selected as sources of good ideas or apparently promising approaches.

The main body of the guide's text contains many 'good practice' points or guidelines. These are derived from the Commission's work, from other accepted guidance (eg from the Housing Corporation), or from CIH's work as the professional body for housing.

How is the guide organised?

Chapter 2 sets the context for the rest of the guide by looking at the changing picture at national and local levels, the Commission's work and especially what is now defined as 'community cohesion' and 'integration', the role of housing organisations and the expectations placed on them by legislation and by regulatory bodies.

Chapter 3 gives important background information about how neighbourhoods are changing – how new migration is affecting the make up of BME communities and what new housing needs have emerged.

The five chapters that form the core of the guide proceed from detail to strategic and organisational issues. The previous guide placed strategic issues first. The order here reflects the fact that housing organisations may want to work immediately on some local issues, at the same time as developing a strategic context. However, those who want to work from 'the top down' might want to read chapters 7 and 8 first.

Chapter 4 looks in detail at how we can build cohesive neighbourhoods, both in removing negative barriers (like tackling hostility between groups and anti-social behaviour) and in positively helping people to integrate (eg new arrivals in a community). It deals with some of the wider issues that arise, such as residential segregation and myth busting about ethnic mix or about newly-arriving groups.

Chapter 5 concerns the mainstream work of housing providers in securing mixed and cohesive neighbourhoods – covering issues such as lettings, supporting people who want to move to unfamiliar areas, and action in the private housing sectors.

Chapter 6 is about achieving cohesion in the context of significant housing-led investment and neighbourhood change, whether this is new development or regeneration of existing neighbourhoods. It emphasises the 'people' element of such change and how this is as important as the buildings or infrastructure.

Chapter 7 places housing in the wider context of local community cohesion strategies, and the obligations of bodies such as Local Strategic Partnerships. Housing organisations may also want to devise their own community cohesion strategies and this chapter describes the steps to follow.

Chapter 8 looks at roles within housing organisations, from board or cabinet level down to those based in and working with communities. It tackles some of the issues that have to be faced organisationally, such as how to ensure that cohesion is reflected in the whole organisation's profile and work and how to develop an effective communications strategy.

Appendices give guidance on two important issues raised in the Singh Commission's report: how community cohesion principles apply to funding of community organisations ('single group funding'), and how they apply to translation and interpreter services.

Terminology

Throughout the guide, the term *community* is used to mean a group of people who share one or more defining characteristics in common, for example ethnicity. The word *neighbourhood* will be used to mean an area containing housing, where there is some degree of agreement by the people who live there about its name and boundaries.

The terms *community cohesion* and *integration* are of course also intrinsic to the guide, but these will be considered in detail in chapter 2.

A *social landlord* is a local authority (where it manages housing stock), an arms length management organisation (ALMO) or a housing association. A *housing organisation* includes all of these bodies but also private developers, estate agents, lettings agencies, private landlords and mortgage lenders.

Cantle report refers to the report published by the Home Office in 2001: *Community Cohesion: Report of the Independent Review Team Chaired by Ted Cantle.*

The term *black and minority ethnic* (BME) is in common usage and will be taken to include the wide range of visible minority groups that make up the population of Britain. It will also include groups that are not always visibly different from the majority white population but who often face disadvantage in housing or who suffer hostility from other people. Some newly-arrived communities (see below) and also established Gypsy and Traveller groups are therefore included within the scope of the term. *Ethnic minority* and *minority ethnic* are used interchangeably with the same meaning as *BME*.

The guide makes a further differentiation between communities of different types, as follows:

- *Long-established communities* – used to refer to groups that have lived in a place for some years, which may themselves also be BME communities (for example, Asian communities established in Britain for thirty years or more). *Long-established 'white' communities* refers to neighbourhoods almost entirely lived in by white people (although few if any places are 100% 'white'); these often include places where BME people have felt unwelcome. Conversely, neighbourhoods largely lived in by BME communities (and sometimes where white people have felt excluded) are called *areas of traditional settlement*.
- *New migrants* – used as an umbrella term to refer to many different groups that have come to Britain in the last few years, including *asylum seekers, refugees* and *migrant workers*.

- *Asylum seekers* are people who have applied for asylum but whose cases have not yet been accepted. They become *refugees* when this has happened and they have been given some form of long-term leave to remain in the UK.
- *Migrant workers* are people who have come primarily to work and may or may not be planning to stay in Britain long-term.

These terms about migration simplify the different categories and more detailed guidance can be found in the CIH/JRF guide *Housing and Support Services for Asylum Seekers and Refugees*[1] and in the web-based resources of the Housing Corporation and CLG-sponsored *Opening Doors* project.[2]

References to the Singh Commission documents

In the guide, the term *Commission* refers to the independent commission appointed by Ruth Kelly in 2006 and chaired by Darra Singh. Information on its work is on its website (www.integrationandcohesion.org.uk). These are the reports produced as part of the Commission's work, and how they are described in the guide:

Report	Referred to as
The Commission's final report *Our Shared Future*, published in June 2007	the *Commission's report*
The Commission's interim report, published in March 2007	the *Commission's interim report*
Detailed examples, published in June 2007 as *Integration and Cohesion Case Studies*	*Integration and Cohesion Case Studies*
A background study *'What Works' in Community Cohesion*, also published in June 2007	*What Works*

These documents and other background research studies are available on the Commission's website.

---

1 Perry, J (2005). CIH for JRF.
2 See www.cih.org/policy/openingdoors/ – the project is run jointly by CIH and hact (Housing Associations' Charitable Trust).

CHAPTER 2

THE BIG PICTURE – COMMUNITY COHESION AND HOUSING ORGANISATIONS

What this chapter is about

- the changing context at national and local levels
- other policies relating to community cohesion
- defining 'integration' and 'community cohesion'
- role of housing organisations in achieving cohesion
- legislative and other requirements
- housing in the local strategic context

The elements of 'the big picture'

This chapter sets the context for the more detailed ones that follow. There are several different elements to the picture. First, there is where we stand in relation to community cohesion, across England, and for this we rely on the Commission's summary. Then we consider a range of recent developments, in the six years since the Cantle report, that affect the policy context for tackling cohesion. Very importantly, the Commission has recommended a new definition of community cohesion, and we set this out.

Then we consider broadly what role housing organisations can play in creating more cohesive communities and working towards the goals set by the Commission. We also look at what is *expected* of them, through the legal and regulatory framework in which they work. Finally, we summarise the local strategic context in which housing and other bodies operate, and how this can help.

A changing context at national and local levels

The Commission makes twelve points to describe what might be called 'the state of community cohesion in England in 2007'. In summary they are:

- People's perceptions of whether they live in cohesive communities are good in most areas.
- But whether a neighbourhood or a local authority area is cohesive or not depends on a range of local factors which differ from place to place.
- In trying to improve cohesion, we have to identify and tackle *all* of the factors that apply in an area, not just one or two.
- Local action needs to focus on *both* changing individual circumstances and perceptions, *and* tackling issues across an area.
- What factors produce more or less cohesion is not a straightforward question. For example:
    - deprivation is an important factor in some areas, but other areas manage to be both deprived *and* cohesive
    - ASB and crime are factors, but we don't yet know how significant they are
    - continuing discrimination suffered by some communities *is* a factor, and must be tackled
    - diversity in an area can mean less cohesion – but only in certain circumstances.
- The impact of immigration is a concern in some areas even though the economic benefits of it have been demonstrated.
- Fair allocation of services (eg housing) is an important issue.
- Cohesion has to be about places that are increasingly complex and diverse, with new arrivals mixed with long-established communities – which are often both white and BME communities.

While problems remain of the kind that led to the Cantle report in 2001, the issues about cohesion now go beyond the circumstances of a few northern, industrial towns to extend to many different areas, and also go beyond questions of race and religion. This led the Commission to recommend changing the definition of what 'cohesion' means, originally set out in the official guidance that followed the Cantle report (see below).

Other policy developments

While the Commission's work and the decisions which will lead from it are the most significant influence on policy, there have been other policy developments since the 2001 Cantle report which also have an important bearing. Some of these are:

Policy on migration

The expansion of the European Union (EU) from 2004, and the decision to allow migrants from the ten accession states to come to the UK to work, have made a great impact in particular parts of the country, some of which had little previous experience of migration or ethnic diversity. Although there is no official government policy on the *integration* of new migrants, the Audit Commission's study *Crossing Borders*[3] has encapsulated many of the issues and the responses needed at local level, and the practical experience that is beginning to develop.

Asylum seekers and refugees

The year 2002 proved to be the peak year for asylum applications by people coming to the UK, and policy has now shifted somewhat away from concerns with controlling numbers towards integration of accepted refugees – as set out in the Home Office's strategy, *Integration Matters* (see page 30). There remain significant issues however about attitudes towards asylum seekers among politicians and the media, and the tendency by some members of the public to use 'asylum seeker' as a general, derogatory label, applied to new migrants more generally. There are still aspects of policy on asylum which cause considerable local problems, eg destitution among asylum seekers whose applications have been rejected but who remain in the country.[4]

Tackling extremism

Extremism has manifested itself both in incidents like the London bombings and the election in several parts of the country of local councillors from extreme right parties. Government now has an action plan on extremism, and a pathfinder fund, both aimed at work with Muslim communities.[5] The Commission recognised these events as part of the context for its work, while saying that (para. 1.5) 'addressing political extremism must be distinguished from addressing issues relating to integration and cohesion'.

Tackling inequality

Inequality is now seen in wider terms than was perhaps the case at the time of the Cantle report, and this is reflected in the government's Equalities Review, and in the creation of the Commission for Equality and Human Rights to replace the Commission for Racial Equality and other bodies. However, there is still an important commitment by government that by 2021 'no-one should be seriously

---

3   Audit Commission (2007) *Crossing Borders*.
4   The CIH (2003) paper *Providing a Safe Haven: Housing Asylum Seekers and Refugees* sets out many of the issues about asylum policy and community cohesion.
5   More details at www.communities.gov.uk/index.asp?id=1506079

disadvantaged by where they live', ie to tackle place-based poverty.[6] This is particularly significant because deprivation may be a factor in preventing communities being cohesive.

The 'Respect' agenda

The government's agenda for tackling crime and ASB is also important in the cohesion context, for many reasons. One is the direct effect which these issues have on whether communities are cohesive (though as we have said this is not clear cut), but also because measures to tackle crime and ASB often interrelate with those to promote cohesion. So, for example, the role of neighbourhood wardens or police community support officers may well be important in cohesion work as well as in tackling ASB.

Community conflict and 'hate' crime

Part of the context for the Cantle report was the slightly earlier (1999) report by William Macpherson on the murder of Stephen Lawrence, which led to policies to tackle 'institutional racism'. Regrettably there have since been other racist murders, including some of asylum seekers. Although there have been no further community-level disturbances on the scale of those in 2001 that led to the Cantle inquiry, there have been more minor ones in Wrexham and Boston (both relating to new migration). One approach to tackling the community racism which fosters such crimes has been the use of community-based mediation methods, based on experience with deeply-divided communities in Northern Ireland.

Sustainable communities and 'place-shaping'

Another policy shift has been to recognise the importance of sustainability and of 'place' across a whole raft of government policy, especially in the fields of housing, regeneration and local government generally. Creating *cohesive* communities has not necessarily been recognised as part of this, however, a point made by the Commission (see below).

Developments in housing policy

Several developments directly relating to housing have included the report on social housing by John Hills (with its emphasis on community mix in terms mainly of *income* and *tenure*), the Cave review of housing regulation (see below), significant investment in both new development and in older areas (eg through the housing market renewal pathfinders), and the preparations for a new government agency to replace the Housing Corporation and English Partnerships. These all represent opportunities to work towards greater cohesion, but equally they could be missed opportunities if cohesion is not factored into the changes being made.

---

6   Social Exclusion Unit (2001) *A New Commitment to Neighbourhood Renewal: National Strategy Action Plan*.

The purpose of referring to these developments in the context of the guide is simply to locate them as part of the context in which housing organisations work, and because they affect policies to improve community cohesion, whether or not the effect is immediately apparent. We will therefore refer throughout the guide to this wider policy context for housing, as well as the framework provided by the Commission's report.

We would emphasise a point made by the Commission, which is that many aspects of government policy (such as these) need to have a 'cohesion' dimension and be judged by whether or not they contribute to cohesion, in addition to whatever other policy objectives they may have.

What do 'community cohesion' and 'integration' mean?

As we pointed out in chapter 1, the terminology used to talk about cohesion emerged from the Cantle report and subsequent guidance.[7] The Commission reviewed the definitions, and those interested in their discussions can look at chapter 2 of their report. They reflect points about some of the shortcomings of the previous definition made by CIH and many other bodies that gave evidence to the Commission.[8] Some of the important conclusions from the debate are:

- Cohesion is the process that must happen in all communities to ensure that different groups of people get on well together, while integration is about ensuring that *new* residents and *existing* ones adapt to each other. These are separate but interlocking concepts.

- Some communities may only need work to promote cohesion, but in others cohesion will not be achieved unless integration is also encouraged. This applies most obviously to areas experiencing change and the ingress of new communities, but it can also apply where pockets within long-established communities have become isolated for different reasons (eg because of language barriers).

- The language around cohesion can be contentious, and there needs to be scope for local communities to arrive at their own interpretations of what cohesion and integration mean in their areas and their own names for the local strategy to achieve the objectives. This has happened, for example, in Tameside (page 31) and Barking and Dagenham (page 123).

So the Commission decided to recommend a new definition, set out overleaf.

---

7   The guidance was that published by the LGA on behalf of a range of official bodies, see LGA (2002) *Guidance on Community Cohesion*. LGA, ODPM, Home Office, CRE and Interfaith Network for the United Kingdom.

8   The CIH's evidence, which will be referred to again in the guide, can be downloaded at www.cih.org/policy/papers3.htm/ohttp://www.cih.org/policy/papers3.htm

---

A new definition of community cohesion

An integrated and cohesive community is one where:

- There is a clearly defined and widely shared sense of the contribution of different individuals and different communities to a future vision for a neighbourhood, city, region or country.

- There is a strong sense of an individual's rights and responsibilities when living in a particular place – people know what everyone expects of them, and what they can expect in turn.

- Those from different backgrounds have similar life opportunities, access to services and treatment.

- There is a strong sense of trust in institutions locally to act fairly in arbitrating between different interests and for their role and justifications to be subject to public scrutiny.

- There is a strong recognition of the contribution of both those who have newly arrived and those who already have deep attachments to a particular place, with a focus on what they have in common.

- There are strong and positive relationships between people from different backgrounds in the workplace, in schools and other institutions within neighbourhoods.

Source: Commission report, para. 3.15

The CIH contribution to the question of defining 'cohesion' and 'integration' made four cautionary points:[9]

- To implement a definition requires ways of collecting intelligence on these issues, including both formal means such as surveys and less formal means such as community forums, etc. There is a need for both good base information and for information showing how circumstances and attitudes change over time.

- Definitions need to be adaptable to local conditions, so that they reflect local priorities and can be developed into an agreed agenda with people in the community itself.

- Any definitions, actions and measures of achievement should include *all* marginalised groups (eg new migrants as well as longer-established BME groups) and more marginalised groups within wider groups (eg Bangladeshi women, or Asian young men).

- Finally, setting all of these factors out in this way might imply a very ambitious task in any given community. However, it is important not to have excessive expectations. Particularly at the level of the individual resident, the aim is that

---

9   CIH evidence to the Commission, p5.

they feel reasonably comfortable and accepted in an area and get on with people, but not that they are necessarily engaged in a range of local groups or are community activists.

These points still apply, and the Commission has rightly emphasised that cohesion is needed in *all* communities, not just those that are racially-mixed. In this context, CIH would comment that the new definition does not (unlike the old one) specifically call for strong and positive relationships *within neighbourhoods themselves*. However, this is implicit in the overall thrust of the Commission's work and is treated as a central theme in this guide.

What opportunities do housing organisations have to help achieve cohesion and integration?

The whole of this guide addresses this question, but it is useful by way of introduction to consider broadly what role housing organisations can play, and how cohesion is (or should be) reflected in their work.

Here are ten reasons why housing's role is a key one.

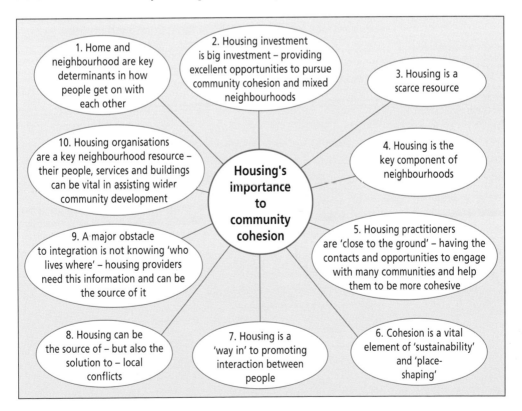

1. Home and neighbourhood are key determinants in how people get on with each other

2. Housing investment is big investment – providing excellent opportunities to pursue community cohesion and mixed neighbourhoods

3. Housing is a scarce resource

10. Housing organisations are a key neighbourhood resource – their people, services and buildings can be vital in assisting wider community development

Housing's importance to community cohesion

4. Housing is the key component of neighbourhoods

9. A major obstacle to integration is not knowing 'who lives where' – housing providers need this information and can be the source of it

5. Housing practitioners are 'close to the ground' – having the contacts and opportunities to engage with many communities and help them to be more cohesive

8. Housing can be the source of – but also the solution to – local conflicts

7. Housing is a 'way in' to promoting interaction between people

6. Cohesion is a vital element of 'sustainability' and 'place-shaping'

1. The importance of home and neighbourhood

The creation of good neighbourhoods provides an important context, perhaps *the* most important context, for the development of knowledge, contact and respect. The home and its immediate surroundings are places where people spend a substantial proportion of their time, even for those who are in paid work outside the home, and they are more 'embracing' environments than many others, such as work places and schools. It is difficult to escape friction in the living environment and tensions are often keenly felt.

2. Housing investment is big investment

Where areas face major change, whether through new developments like the Thames Gateway, or through more modest development schemes, or through regeneration programmes like New Deal for Communities or the housing market renewal pathfinders, the housing element in the investment is invariably a major one and often the one that has most impact on people's lives.

Such investment provides an opportunity to tackle wider problems than just increasing the number of houses available or dealing with obsolete property. Investment opportunities can be used positively to help develop more cohesive communities – or preserve ones that already exist. Conversely, handled wrongly, they can miss that opportunity or even make tensions worse and increase the isolation which some communities feel.

3. Housing is a scarce resource

Housing organisations are vital in achieving more cohesive communities for many reasons. First, because housing practitioners both work with existing communities and help build new ones, they are among the professionals whose work is most crucial in determining whether those communities are successful. Second, housing is also a highly-valued commodity and in many parts of the country is in high demand. Housing can easily become the spark point for conflict between people or communities. As Steve Douglas, Acting Chief Executive of the Housing Corporation and a member of the Commission, said in a speech which announced this guide:

> '*Housing policy has the potential to contribute positively to integration and cohesion – and is one of the key areas in which integration and cohesion should be mainstreamed. But with housing a scarce resource, it also has the capacity to be a key bone of contention in our communities.*'

Third, housing organisations in all sectors have a responsibility to be fair in their role as 'gatekeepers' to housing as a scarce resource, to be transparent in the way they allocate, let or sell property, and to dispel – rather than fuel – the myths that develop about who is entitled to what. This applies equally in areas with very strong demand for housing and in those where the market is much less pressured but there is still scope for one community to feel that another is being favoured at its expense.

4. Housing is the key component of neighbourhoods

Although many things shape a neighbourhood, such as the mix of people living there, the ways in which they interact and the contribution made by institutions like local schools, the neighbourhood would not exist without the houses. Who lives in them, how they gain access to them and whether or not the houses are well looked after affect all residents in an area. The social composition of a neighbourhood is a key determinant of the composition of the users of local facilities, particularly schools but also local health and leisure facilities.

The availability of opportunities for people to move into the area (or move within the area and stay near family or friends) also affect the cohesiveness of an area because *where* we live is so important to all of us. Housing professionals in all sectors shape or influence the housing market in an area and therefore the impact it has on communities living there.

5. Housing practitioners are 'close to the ground'

Whereas a range of professionals such as police and teachers also have day-to-day contact with communities, in some neighbourhoods housing practitioners are the ones who have most regular contact, whether as housing managers, officers dealing with conditions in the private rented sector, or providers of neighbourhood-based services such as caretakers and neighbourhood wardens. This gives them the local intelligence, the contacts and the opportunities to engage with communities in those areas and help them to be more cohesive.

The other side of this coin is that, for residents, contact with housing staff may be one of the most frequent forms of contact they have with official bodies of any kind, whether individually in reporting disrepair or collectively through a residents' or tenants' organisation. The ways they organise locally to deal with housing issues can also provide the means for tackling wider issues in the area that bear on how cohesive the community is, or on how conflicts can be resolved which affect the community.

6. Cohesion is a vital element of 'sustainability' and 'place-shaping'

Housing organisations operate within a wider local and regional context – they might be part of Local Strategic Partnerships, be partners in sub-regional programmes such as housing market renewal, or be engaged in a strategic housing role with regional bodies such as the Regional Development Agency. In addition, the government is charging local authorities and regional bodies with a broader 'place-shaping' remit and with making a significant contribution to its Sustainable Communities Plan.

The Commission report argues that community cohesion should be an objective at all these levels, and a test of the policies that emerge. It says that it should be an integral part of building sustainable communities and of successful place-shaping. Housing bodies are well-placed both to help ensure that this happens and to contribute to debates and policies from their on-the-ground experience of cohesion issues. We return to this in more detail at the end of this chapter.

7. Housing is a 'way in' to promoting interaction between people

One of the key themes of the earlier Cantle report and reflected in the Commission's report is what Cantle identified as people leading 'parallel lives' – the classic case of (say) an Asian and a white community adjacent to each other in the same town, but with practically no interaction between them. Although the Commission rightly says that the challenge of cohesion now goes beyond these circumstances, nevertheless getting people from different communities to interact positively remains a key element.

Housing organisations can promote this in many ways. For example, it may not be enough simply to ensure that everyone has equal access to housing in certain areas, steps may be needed to break down the real or perceived barriers to people moving into unfamiliar areas. The extent to which this happens successfully is bound to affect success in promoting interaction elsewhere, eg between young people and within schools. Where people live does not determine whether they will interact, but it can act as a great barrier to interaction in certain circumstances.

8. Housing can be the source of – but also the solution to – local conflicts

Although we noted that housing is a scarce resource, many of the conflicts that occur at community level are about more mundane issues such as whether houses are looked after or not, litter, vandalism and problems between neighbours (such as noisy parties). Housing practitioners are often in a position both to find out about such problems and help solve them. For example, many of the studies of the impact of recent migration of workers, from the EU accession states, have pointed to the impact of their poor living conditions, overcrowding and the effect of privately-let properties on the rest of a neighbourhood. Both the agents involved in letting and managing property, and the local authority staff responsible for controlling conditions in privately-let property, can help in solving these problems and prevent them becoming (as they have in some places) a source of major tension.

9. A major obstacle to integration is not knowing 'who lives where'

Particularly in areas of recent migration, a serious obstacle faced by all service providers is lack of information about new communities, where they live and the difficulties they face (such as language barriers). As Steve Douglas said:

'We also need to better understand and consider the mix and churn of local areas. Who is actually living in our communities and neighbourhoods? What are their aspirations? What are their needs?'

Housing providers both need this information and can be a source of it, either through their own monitoring (eg of allocations or use of advice services), or through surveys or links with local community groups and community development workers.

10. Housing organisations are a key neighbourhood resource

Finally, the people, services and buildings and other resources which housing organisations have within neighbourhoods can be a vital resource in assisting the wider development of the community, of which cohesion is a component part.

Housing associations, for example, have been involved in a range of initiatives which go far beyond the narrow 'landlord' role – bringing together disparate groups within an area (eg young and old), making buildings available as community facilities, and providing start-up help to new community organisations. This role of associations as 'community anchors' is already growing.[10]

How are housing organisations *expected* to contribute?

All housing organisations are subject to the laws on discrimination and promoting equality, and to regulatory requirements which may relate to promoting cohesion and integration. In addition, expectations may be placed on them indirectly, eg as a condition of receiving public funds. What follows is a summary of expectations that relate to cohesion and integration. It should not be relied on as an interpretation of the law.

Legal requirements under race relations legislation

Section 71 of the Race Relations Act 1996 – amended by the Race Relations (Amendment) Act 2000 and extended to a wider range of public sector bodies – states that public sector bodies shall, in carrying out their functions:

'have due regard to the need – (a) to eliminate unlawful discrimination; and (b) to promote equality of opportunity and good relations between persons of different racial groups.'

The last element – promoting good race relations – has the most relevance to community cohesion.

---

10   See Wadhams, C (2006) *An Opportunity Waiting to Happen: Housing associations as 'community anchors'*. Hact/NHF.

Section 71 applies to a number of bodies that have housing responsibilities, including local authorities and the Housing Corporation, and also to the Scottish Government, Communities Scotland and the Welsh Assembly Government. If a listed public authority has a contract or other arrangement with a private company or a voluntary organisation to carry out any of its functions, and the duty applies to those functions, the authority is responsible for meeting the duty concerning those functions. This brings housing associations and ALMOs within the scope of the legislation.

The general duty does not tell public authorities how to do their work, but it expects them to assess whether race equality is relevant to their functions.

Detailed guidance on the statutory duties is available.[11]

Guidance on promoting good race relations

The official guidance in implementing the 'positive duty' to promote good race relations in housing includes several points relevant to cohesion and integration, for example:

- encourage dialogue among people from all racial groups on how well local housing polices and services are working
- make sure people from all racial groups take part in decision-making about housing services
- make sure the needs of people from all racial groups are catered for, and work with other organisations to help deliver these services
- monitor patterns in the development of racial tensions concerning the provision of housing
- take firm and immediate action to deal with incidents of racial harassment
- make sure that housing allocation policies maximise opportunities for people from all racial groups to interact, and do not effectively lead to segregation of racial groups.

More extensive guidance is available in the statutory *Code of Practice on Race Equality in Housing*, a new version of which was published in 2006 (separate versions are available for England, Scotland and Wales). It shows how the principles of promoting good relations and community cohesion inter-relate.

Most public authorities, including all local authorities, CLG and the Housing Corporation, are required to produce a 'race equality scheme' which sets out how they plan to carry out their duties and monitor their performance in implementing the act,

---

11 From the Commission for Racial Equality, at www.cre.gov.uk – whose duties are taken over by the Commission for Equality and Human Rights, as explained below.

and the schemes should take account of this official advice. CLG has a race equality scheme which makes considerable reference to its policies on community cohesion.[12] The race equality duties were joined in 2006 and 2007 respectively by similar duties relating to disability and gender, and these are often treated together in overall equality schemes.

Each scheme must include the ways in which the body will assess the impact of what they do on race, disability or gender equality. Such assessments are called 'equality impact assessments'. One recommendation from the Commission's report (para. 8.33) is that these assessments should in future cover the impact of policies on integration and cohesion.

In Scotland, both the Scottish Government and Communities Scotland have equality strategies, and the Scottish Government has a race equality scheme.[13] None of these has a strong community cohesion element, however. The issue tends to be dealt with by subject area, so for example there is a Scottish Refugee Integration Forum and *Action Plan*, and there is a 'Fresh Talent' campaign to encourage people to come to live in Scotland.[14] Similarly, the Welsh Assembly Government has a race equality scheme, a *Refugee Housing Action Plan* and has a draft BME housing strategy.[15]

Wider requirements and changing duties on 'equality'

The government is in the process of reviewing its whole mechanism for delivering greater equality in society. It has carried out an 'Equalities Review' and is bringing together the different official bodies into a single Commission for Equality and Human Rights (which begins work in October, 2007).[16]

It is now also reviewing and consolidating the law on equality and discrimination. Its consultation[17] makes clear that it intends to build on the 'good relations' element of race discrimination law, and the requirement to promote 'positive attitudes' in disability discrimination law, to create a broad duty on public bodies requiring them to:

- Address disadvantage – take steps to counter the effects of disadvantage experienced by groups protected by discrimination law, so as to place people on an equal footing with others.
- Promote respect for the equal worth of different groups, and fostering good relations within and between groups – take steps to treat people with dignity

---

12   Available at www.communities.gov.uk/index.asp?id=1500184
13   See www.communitiesscotland.gov.uk
14   See www.scotland.gov.uk/Topics/Government/Promoting-Scotland/18738
15   See http://new.wales.gov.uk/topics/equality/?lang=en
16   See its website (www.cehr.org.uk) for further details.
17   CLG (2007) *A Framework for Fairness: Proposals for a Single Equality Bill for Great Britain*.

and respect and to promote understanding of diversity and mutual respect between groups, which is a prerequisite for strong, cohesive communities.

- Meet different needs while promoting shared values – take steps to meet the particular needs of different groups, while at the same time delivering functions in ways which emphasise shared values rather than differences and which provide opportunities for sustained interactions within and between groups.
- Promote equal participation – take steps to involve excluded or under-represented groups in employment and decision-making structures and processes and to promote equal citizenship.

This duty would apply to issues of race, gender and disability and, subject to consultation, may extend to age, sexual orientation and religion or belief. Such changes are likely (as with the current law) to be implemented in part through the regulatory and performance regimes (in housing, currently through the Housing Corporation and the Audit Commission, and their equivalents in Scotland and Wales).

There is a useful summary of the main legislation on equality and diversity issues as at the end of 2006, issued by the Audit Commission (downloadable at http://snipurl.com/supdiversity).

The government's target for community cohesion

The government currently has a range of targets, called Public Service Agreements (PSAs) which relate to the government's main objectives and departmental responsibilities. The Department for Communities and Local Government has ten such targets of which the last, PSA 10, is to reduce perceptions of racial discrimination and increase perceptions of community cohesion. (There is currently no PSA relating to integration, eg of migrants or refugees).

CLG has to report on its progress in meeting its PSA targets; the latest report on PSA 10 was in 2007.[18] The cohesion aspect is assessed through a question in the two-yearly Citizenship Survey, which asks people if they agree that their local area is one where people from different backgrounds get on well together. In the last two surveys (2003 and 2005) 80 per cent have agreed that it is. (The Commission's report[19] looks at these results in more detail and we return to this issue in chapter 7.)

In housing, CLG relies on the delivery agencies – mainly local authorities (and their ALMOs, if they have them) and housing associations – for progress in achieving PSA 10. These social landlords are expected to comply with a range of non-statutory

18   CLG (2007) *Improving Opportunity, Strengthening Society: Two years on*.
19   Commission report, chapter 2.

requirements or assessments that together constitute their 'performance regime'. This is a complex area which is currently under review,[20] so only the key elements (in the English system) which have a bearing on community cohesion are included in the next two sub-sections.

Elements of the performance regime for local housing authorities

- *Comprehensive Performance Assessment (CPA)*. Local authorities are subject to CPAs across the full range of their services. The CPA looks at each authority's overall performance in establishing a vision for its community and pursuing objectives such as sustainability and community safety. If an authority is performing badly in relation to community cohesion, this could affect its CPA performance rating.

- *Comprehensive Area Assessments (CAAs)*. These will replace CPAs in 2009, and among other elements will have a stronger focus on community cohesion. Although the detail is still being developed, the Commission has called (para. 4.27) for CAAs to incorporate clear, locally-determined measures of integration and cohesion, which recognise varied experiences at local level.

- *Inspections of local authorities and ALMOs*. While every local authority is subject to a CPA, inspections of housing services take place only in certain circumstances. For example, there are regular inspections of ALMOs because of the extra investment resources they receive. These inspections take into account both performance indicators and KLOEs (see below), and therefore will (among many other things) take account of the organisation's performance in promoting community cohesion.

- *Key Lines of Inquiry (KLOEs)*. KLOEs are tools used in Audit Commission inspections, including those of local authorities, ALMOs and housing associations (see below). KLOE 31 covers 'Diversity', and specifically asks if the organisation promotes community cohesion. It sets tests that an 'excellent' housing organisation would meet in responding to this question, including the arrangements it would have for monitoring its performance.[21]

- *Best Value Performance Indicators (BVPIs)*. These are set nationally and are intended to enable comparison between organisations on key, measurable outcomes. Some specifically address issues of services to BME customers (eg BV164 – 'Does the organisation follow the CRE Code of Practice in rented housing?'). There are also 'corporate health' indicators which are relevant, such as BV2a on the Equality Standard for Local Government, or BV2 on the duty to promote race equality.

---

20   As a result of the Cave Review and consultation on the setting up of Communities England.
21   See the Audit Commission web pages on KLOEs at www.audit-commission.gov.uk/kloe/

- *Performance indicators (PIs).* Organisations are encouraged to develop and measure their own local PIs. One suggested by government is the local equivalent of the national PSA on community cohesion, ie. the percentage of people who feel their local area is a place where people from different backgrounds get on well together.[22]

Elements of the performance regime for housing associations

Housing associations have their own regulatory regime administered (in England) by the Housing Corporation, of which one element is a similar system of inspection (by the Audit Commission) as the one that applies to local authorities.

- *The Regulatory Code.* The Corporation's overall approach is set out in its Regulatory Code, which is based on three broad areas of activity – viability, governance and management. This states that associations:

    '...must work towards the elimination of discrimination and demonstrate an equitable approach to the rights and responsibilities of individuals. They must promote good relations between people of different racial groups'. Housing Corporation Regulatory Code para. 2.7.

- *Guidance.* The Corporation publishes guidance on different aspects of the code. Equality and diversity issues are covered in *Good Practice Note 8.*

- *Housing Corporation Assessments (HCAs).* HAs with over 250 properties are subject to regular assessments which reflect their performance in relation to the code. This is expressed in terms of 'traffic lights' relating to the three broad areas noted above plus performance in housing development.

- *Equalities Schemes and Community Cohesion Strategy.* The Corporation has race, gender and disability equality schemes, and a community cohesion strategy (developed in parallel with this guide). The Corporation expects HAs to have regard to policies such as these and to show how their own policies, practices and governance arrangements reflect them.

- *Affordable Housing Programme.* The Corporation's investment programme encourages providers of new housing to cater for all communities, and to work with BME housing associations and refugee community organisations. The Corporation's prospectus for its *National Affordable Housing Programme 2008-11* requires those bidding for the programme to include a method statement, in relevant areas, showing how they plan to meet the needs of minority communities and promote community cohesion, and how they have engaged with local community organisations.[23]

---

22 See Home Office (2003) *Building a Picture of Community Cohesion.* Performance indicators are covered in more detail in chapter 6 of the guide.

23 Housing Corporation (2007), pp 22-24.

- *Performance Inspections*. The performance of associations in delivering services is subject to inspections by the Audit Commission, which (in part) uses KLOEs and PIs (see above) to inform its reports. HAs (like LAs) are able to develop their own PIs, for example on community cohesion and integration.

Current policy on community cohesion

Although this guide is based around the work of the Singh Commission, in the expectation that this will shape future policy in this field, *current* policy on community cohesion is set out in a range of documents. The sheer number and varied sources of these can be confusing. For convenience, the main ones that are still current are listed and briefly described in the box on page 30.

These documents, predating the Commission's report, will be referred to in the guide where particularly relevant. (Readers should note that departmental responsibility for cohesion was changed in May, 2006, from the Home Office to CLG. Many of these documents predate this change).

How does work on community cohesion and housing fit with wider policies at local level?

The government is making wide-ranging reforms as a result of the local government white paper published in 2006.[24] These changes will affect all aspects of a local authority's strategic and 'place-shaping' roles. The key elements and their relevance to community cohesion are described below.

Housing organisations may not necessarily be involved directly in these – but they may have opportunities to contribute, especially to 'thematic partnerships' and to Local Area Agreements where these impact on housing or on neighbourhoods where social landlords are key agencies.

Sustainable Community Strategies and 'Place-Shaping'

The Sustainable Community Strategy creates a long-term, sustainable vision for an area, to be agreed between the local authority and its major partners (through the LSP – see below). The government wants authorities to concentrate the strategy on 'place-shaping' – described in the Lyons report on local authority finance as:[25]

'...creative use of powers and influence to promote the general well-being of a community and its citizens.'

---

24   CLG (2006) *Strong and Prosperous Communities*.
25   See www.lyonsinquiry.org.uk para. 2.43

Current policy documents on Community Cohesion – Summary

Building a Picture of Community Cohesion   *Home Office, 2003*
- provides guidance on establishing indicators of community cohesion and collecting data to measure them.

Building Community Cohesion into Area-Based Initiatives   *Home Office, 2004*
- advises those engaged in regeneration programmes on how to ensure they lead to greater community cohesion
- suggests tests that should be applied to 'area-based initiatives' from the cohesion perspective.

Community Cohesion: An action guide   *LGA (with the Home Office, ODPM, CRE, Audit Commission, etc), 2004*

- updates the 2002 *Guidance on Community Cohesion*
- advises on building up local information
- proposes indicators of success in achieving community cohesion
- has numerous practical examples and local contacts
- sets out LA obligations under race equality legislation
- encourages engagement of local communities
- advises on dealing with the media and on 'myth busting'.

Community Cohesion: Seven Steps – A practitioner's toolkit   *Home Office/ODPM, 2005*
- toolkit based on the experience of the earlier 'pathfinder' programme, with many practical examples
- complements the *Action Guide* (see above) by being aimed at a wider audience

---

Leading Cohesive Communities: A guide for local authority leaders and chief executives
IDeA/LGA, 2006
- aimed at achieving the commitment of local government leaders
- looks at the key strategic issues facing local authorities

Improving Opportunity, Strengthening Society: Two years on   *CLG, 2007*
- appraisal of progress in race equality and community cohesion against government policy targets
- updates policy and gives practical examples

Integration Matters   *Home Office, 2005*
- sets out government policy on refugee integration
- has suggested indicators on refugee integration
- makes plans for specific services to assist integration, such as the Sunrise programme (due to be rolled out nationally in 2008)
- followed by a more detailed paper *A New Model for National Refugee Integration Services* (2006).

Note: all the above (except *Integration Matters*, available from the Home Office website) can be downloaded at www.communities.gov.uk/index.asp?id=1502397

Lyons went on to say that:[26]

> '...*engagement and action by authorities can provide the connections for integration and cohesion by developing trust and mutual respect within the wider community, building community identity and pride in place, and developing relationships between citizens in a community...It has not been something that local authorities have always seen as part of their role.*'

Both the white paper (para. 8.32) and the Commission's report (para. 4.24) said that an area's strategy should make explicit reference to integration and community cohesion, and there is detailed guidance on this in *Leading Cohesive Communities*. Some areas have already done these things – for example, Tameside (see box).

More details on the new approach to preparing Sustainable Community Strategies, reflecting these changes, will be published early in 2008.

Tameside Community Cohesion Partnership

A 'Building Stronger Communities' event in Tameside was attended by more than 100 members of the public. The IDeA worked with Tameside MBC and the Tameside Community Cohesion Partnership to design and delivery this multi-sector event that included exhibitions, competitions and a range of involvement techniques. It allowed people to:

- define what the words 'community cohesion' actually mean for them
- articulate what they like and dislike about Tameside, the trigger points for conflict and tension in the future
- express their hopes and concerns for the future of communities in Tameside
- work together with others to build a vision for stronger, supportive communities and community cohesion
- identify key issues and actions for organisations and individuals
- highlight examples of people who could be regarded as 'community cohesion role models', that participants would like to 'Invite to tea' to discuss cohesion issues.

The event engaged faith communities, community activists and vulnerable groups such as young people in care, older adults and traditionally-excluded groups such as black women. The emerging priorities were woven into the Sustainable Community Strategy for Tameside and corporate priorities for the council. The key message from the day was 'don't be afraid to challenge bigotry and stand up for what you believe in'.

Source: *Leading Cohesive Communities*

---

26   Para. 2.64.

Local Strategic Partnerships (LSPs)

Local Strategic Partnerships are overall bodies created to bring together the three sectors (public, private, voluntary) to set a 'strategic vision' for the local authority area, lead the drive to improve public services and address the government's wider 'sustainable communities' agenda. LSPs have a lead role in – and may draw up – the Sustainable Community Strategy and Local Area Agreement(s). As well as this overall role, LSPs also include 'thematic partnerships' on issues such as crime prevention, improving the health of the community, and so on.

Several LSPs (eg Peterborough and Boston) have established thematic partnerships on community cohesion, or ensured that their partnerships take account of cohesion in tacking other issues such as crime. There are case studies of LSPs and community cohesion in the ORRION toolkit.[27] At the same time, LSPs have also been criticised in research by the CRE for failing to secure sufficient ethnic minority involvement in the partnerships, or to pursue race equality objectives.[28]

Local Area Agreements (LAAs)

An LAA is a three-year agreement, based on the local Sustainable Community Strategy, and made between central government, represented by the Government Office (GO), and a local area, represented by the lead local authority and other key partners through LSPs.

From 2008 each authority will have a single LAA which will combine many of the authority's existing funding streams. LAAs will be set on the basis of a range of targets agreed with GOs. These will include 'improvement targets', which might be drawn from national performance indicators or might be purely local targets. Government has said that it will:[29]

> '...work with local authorities and their partners to identify those places where cohesion should be a local priority reflected in improvement targets in Local Area Agreements (LAAs) and work with them on how they should address local challenges.'

Agencies have already come together to agree priorities and share budgets in order to address 'cross-cutting' issues in the previous version of LAAs. Some adopted themes relevant to cohesion – for example, Leicester's LAA cross-cutting theme was *Community Cohesion – Learning to Live Together*. Given the part which cohesion and integration should play in each local Sustainable Community Strategy, they should also be an integral component of the LAA.

---

27   ORRION is the 'online race resource for improving outcomes in neighbourhood renewal'. See www.renewal.net/toolkits/orriontoolkit/
28   See www.cre.gov.uk/research/localstrategicpartnerships.html
29   In the local government white paper, para. 8.8

Checklist on regulation and performance issues

✓ Is someone in the organisation 'in charge' of community cohesion issues? – senior enough to be able to make things happen?

✓ Is community cohesion reflected in the organisation's policies and practices on equality and diversity?

✓ Is your organisation planning for the forthcoming changes in equality law?

✓ If your organisation is a social landlord, is it familiar with the Audit Commission's KLOE on diversity issues and is it acting to be an excellent organisation in this field?

✓ How can community cohesion be made a key issue in the Sustainable Community Strategy and/or the Local Area Agreement in the area(s) where you work?

THE CHANGING FACE OF NEIGHBOURHOODS

What this chapter is about:

- changes in BME communities
- impact of immigration
- Britain's foreign-born population
- implications for housing and housing providers

The 'new diversity' of the UK population and what it means

One of the most important messages from the Singh Commission is that housing organisations have to adjust to the 'new diversity' of the communities with whom they are working. Although it has always been a simplification to view people as either 'white' or 'black and minority ethnic' this is now even more the case, because of the changes in the population over the last few years. Indeed, some of the most significant changes are so recent that the last (2001) census did not record them.

This chapter aims to give a very short introduction to these issues, for readers who feel that they are not up-to-date. At the end it gives the sources of information for those who need to understand the picture in more depth.

Overall changes in ethnic minority communities

The UK population is now almost 60.6 million people. Within this total, the ethnic minority population is nearly 5m, or 8%.

BME communities in England have changed significantly over the last 20 years. In 1981, Indian, Black Caribbean and Pakistani communities accounted for 63% of the BME population. In 2003, these same groups accounted for 49%. There are new migrant communities emerging in many parts of the country that have few social or cultural similarities to longer-established BME groups.

Overall impact of migration

The UK population is expected to grow to about 67m by 2030, before stabilising. Migration has accounted for about half of Britain's population growth in the last ten years. It is expected to form a *bigger* proportion of population growth up to 2030: of the 7m increase in population, 4m will come from migration and 3m from natural change.

In 2005, about 185,000 more people migrated *into* Britain than migrated *out* (see fig. 1). The previous year had been a record since figures started to be collected in 1991. However, these may not be long-term trends, but are probably related to the expansion of the European Union. In the past, the level of migration has fluctuated considerably. But for the moment, the gap between 'inflow' and 'outflow' is wider than before.

The number of migrant workers coming to Britain from the new countries that have joined the EU is not known, but is believed to be over 400,000 since 2004 (the nationality most represented being Polish). However, many of these migrants have stayed only for a short time to do seasonal work – although there does seem to be a trend for more migrant workers to want to live in the UK on a longer-term basis. In the net inflows shown in Figure 1, the numbers from the 'accession states' account for 49,000 in 2004 and 64,000 in 2005 – a significant share of the totals but much less than the headline figures might suggest.

Figure 1: Recent UK Migration

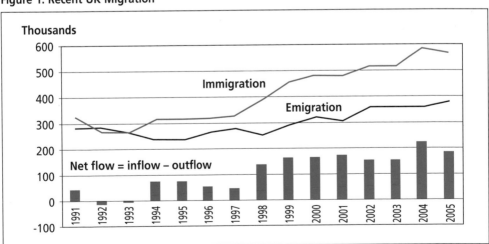

Source: www.statistics.gov.uk

The foreign-born population

These trends mean that one in every twelve people in Britain is now foreign-born (see Figure 2). While about half of these describe themselves as 'white'; the other foreign-born people now join the BME population. Of the total BME population of 4.6m in 2001, half were born outside Britain and half were born here.[30]

In 2004, figures on all the foreign nationals living the UK show that 'traditional' migrant groups such as people from Ireland and India are still at the top of the list, along with others from mainly better-off countries such as the USA, Germany and France. But also in the 'top 20' are much poorer countries such as Zimbabwe (no.11), Somalia (no.13) and Turkey (no.16).

Figure 2: Foreign-born as a percentage of UK population

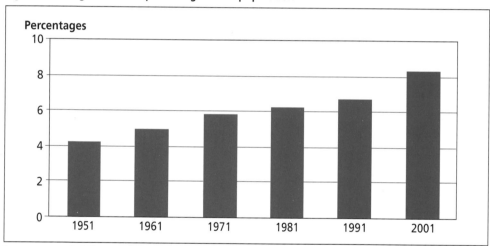

Source: www.statistics.gov.uk

Impact on aspects of life in the UK

Growing diversity is reflected in a number of different factors about life in the UK, for example:

- *Legal status* – migrants vary widely in their legal status. There may be wide differences *within* groups of the same national origin. For example, among Somalis in the UK – and in any single town or city – we will find British citizens, refugees, asylum-seekers, persons granted exceptional leave to remain, undocumented migrants (often people who have stayed beyond the period

---

30   The terms 'white' and 'BME' are used here as they are in official statistics, not in the wider sense we described in chapter 1.

allowed), and people granted refugee status in another European country but who subsequently moved (legally) to Britain.

- *Languages spoken* – in London schools, children speak in total about 300 different 'home' languages. As an example of the changing population picture, in Tower Hamlets, which has a large Sylheti-speaking Bangladeshi population, the demand for East European language services now exceeds that for Sylheti.

- *Religion* – while many migrants come from countries with a Christian background, all the other major religions are of course also represented. An important element in the new diversity of the population is that people may come from different traditions within Christianity, Islam, etc. Somali people may want separate religious facilities to people from (say) Pakistan, even though both communities are traditionally Muslim.

- *Population make-up* – new migrants tend to be younger (concentrated in the 25-44 age group), and to be more male than female – a reversal of the pattern of migration a decade ago. (One consequence is that migrants are helping to rebalance the country's population, which is of course aging.)

- *Reasons for coming here* – there are now about 1.4m foreign workers in the UK and over 300,000 foreign students. Around 100,000 people are granted settlement each year as relatives (mainly spouses and children) of people already living here. Numbers of new asylum seekers peaked at about 80,000 in 2002 but have since declined to about 25,000 annually. In 2006, about 42,000 asylum seekers were receiving state support (numbers not receiving state support are not known). Finally, the Home Office estimates that there could be between 310,000 and 570,000 undocumented migrants in the UK in total.

- *Rich and poor* – overall, the BME population is poorer than the UK average. Groups with the highest levels of poverty are Bangladeshis, Pakistanis and Black Africans ('poor' in this context meaning earnings less than 60% of average earnings). In Bangladeshi communities, almost two-thirds are poor. With Bangladeshi and other groups, poverty is partly the result of larger families being dependent on one or two wage earners. But poverty is also a reflection both of higher unemployment among BME people and of lower pay rates for those with jobs.

Growing diversity has considerable implications for community cohesion, which will be discussed in the guide. These range from the sudden changes that can take place in neighbourhoods as new groups move in, to the interactions (sometimes problematic) between different minority communities, to the changing expectations of younger people in minority communities, particularly those born in the UK who in many cases may still feel that they are not fully accepted as British. There is a much wider range of needs and circumstances, which vary from place to place across Britain, than there was twenty years ago.

Ethnic minorities, housing and neighbourhoods

The wider differences just discussed are also reflected in looking at housing. For example:

- *Tenure* – There are marked differences in tenure between ethnic groups. Indian households are more likely to be owner occupiers than any other ethnic group – including whites. Pakistani households are nearly as likely to own their home as whites are. Bangladeshi and Black African households are less likely to be owners, and more likely to be in social housing. Only ten per cent of Bangladeshi households are private renters, while at the other extreme, 39 per cent of Chinese households are private renters. Although there is limited national information, new EU migrants appear to be highly concentrated in the private rented sector.

- *Social renting* – BME people are more likely than average to be living in social housing, but this also masks big differences between groups and areas. For example, the mainly south Asian communities in Rochdale and Bradford make little use of social housing, while central Manchester and Leeds both have high concentrations of mainly Black African or Black Caribbean people in social housing. Lettings to BME people have been increasing across the social rented sector since 2000.

- *Poor housing conditions* – BME people are more likely to experience bad conditions such as overcrowding, non-decent housing or homelessness, and are more likely to be dissatisfied with their housing.

- *Poor neighbourhoods* – BME people are three times more likely to be living in areas of multiple deprivation, and four times more likely to be in one of the 40 most deprived local authority areas.

- *New migrants typically have the worst conditions* – These include poor quality and overcrowded accommodation in the private rented sector, unsafe neighbourhoods, insecurity because accommodation is tied to jobs, and susceptibility to becoming destitute because many groups do not have access to welfare benefits or homelessness services.

- *Converging housing aspirations?* – on the other hand, second and third generation BME households appear to be more mobile, less likely to want to stay in traditional settlement areas and more open to opportunities such as low cost home ownership. They also seem to be establishing smaller households with less emphasis on keeping extended families together (and less willingness than before by younger households to look after aging parents).

Differences in entitlements to housing and other services

One result of the controls on asylum and on economic migration that the government has introduced in the last few years is a growing complexity of entitlements to services, depending on immigration status. For example, some kinds of migrant are admitted to Britain on the basis of having 'no recourse to public funds', which in most cases debars them from welfare benefits such as housing benefit for an initial period (including, for example, foreign spouses of British citizens). Most asylum seekers are debarred from local authority housing, or from receiving a nomination from a local authority to a housing association. But many people debarred in this way would still (in theory) be eligible for direct housing by an association from its own lettings.

The guide is not the place to explain the details of eligibility, which are set out elsewhere (see resource list at end of chapter). It is however most important that housing organisations ensure that they are correctly informed and that they keep up-to-date with changes. Apart from the effect on potential customers, if they are poorly informed they run the risk of breaching discrimination law by failing to consider someone on the false assumption that they are not entitled to a service (such as being treated as homeless).

The policy of putting increasing restrictions on eligibility for services and even (in the case of most asylum seekers) preventing them from working has an effect on community cohesion. This is because it is an important factor in the growing problem of destitution (for example, of asylum seekers whose cases have been refused, or of certain types of EU migrant who are only eligible for benefits if they are working). Destitution is dealt with in chapter 4.

Implications for housing providers

This chapter is only a brief overview of the way Britain is changing, but (in addition to the 'community cohesion' challenge) it is clearly vital that housing providers respond to these developments. Some of the requirements are:

- *Be aware of changes happening nationally* – and consider their likely implications for housing needs and the responses needed by housing providers.

- *Understand the local impact of the changes* – one of the key messages is that it is no longer possible (if it ever was) to make assumptions about BME communities and their needs based on national data. Local data and intelligence about different kinds of needs, and the way changing communities relate to each other, are vital.

- *Know about national policy and how it alters* – there have been major changes in legislation on migration and on asylum on an almost annual basis, and this is likely to continue. Many of the changes affect the entitlements of new migrants or impose duties on local authorities and housing providers.

- *Keep up to date with good practice as it emerges* – for example, on housing and related services for refugees and new migrants, through the work of the hact, CIH, Housing Corporation and CLG *Opening Doors* project (see below).

- *Ensure that staff are properly trained and briefed* – so that they understand the broad issues (as in this chapter) but also are sufficiently familiar with the details of entitlement to housing and related services, so as not to debar people who may be eligible for help.

More detailed information on the issues in this chapter can be found in the documents or websites listed in the box below. (These are the sources for the facts summarised in the chapter.)

Sources of more detailed information on material in this chapter

Issue	Information source
Population trends	www.statistics.gov.uk www.gad.gov.uk/Population/
Overall changes in BME communities	Harrison, M and Phillips, D (2003) *Housing and BME Communities: Review of the evidence base* (www.communities.gov.uk/index.asp?id=1155611)
Migration – overall	www.statistics.gov.uk www.bbc.co.uk (go to the 'Born Abroad' pages)
Migration – migrant workers	Spencer, S *et al* (2007) *Migrants' Lives Beyond the Workplace – the experiences of Central and East Europeans in the UK* (www.jrf.org.uk)
Foreign-born population – characteristics	Vertovec, S (2007) *New complexities of cohesion in Britain* (www.integrationandcohesion.org.uk)
BME people – poverty and economic circumstances	Platt, L (2007) *Poverty and Ethnicity in the UK* (www.jrf.org.uk)
BME people – housing circumstances	*English House Condition Survey* www.communities.gov.uk/index.asp?id=1155269 Harrison and Phillips – see above
Asylum seekers and refugees – housing and support needs	Perry, J (2005) *Housing and Support Services for Asylum Seekers and Refugees*. CIH. Also the *Opening Doors* website: www.cih.org/policy/openingdoors/
New migrants – housing needs and neighbourhood effects	www.cih.org/policy/openingdoors/ Robinson, D and Reeve, K (2006) *Neighbourhood Experiences of New Migration* (www.jrf.org.uk)
Entitlements to housing and related benefits	An explanatory website is being developed by CIH and hact that will be operational during 2007 – see www.cih.org for details when available.

CHAPTER 4

CREATING STRONG AND POSITIVE RELATIONSHIPS WITHIN NEIGHBOURHOODS

What this chapter is about:

- the elements of a 'cohesive community'
- valuing different contributions
- basic shared values and expectations
- creating equal opportunities
- fair allocation of resources
- welcoming new arrivals and helping people cope with change
- building positive relationships between people from different backgrounds

What are the elements of a 'cohesive community'?

The Commission's new definition of cohesion contains six elements. In summary, these are:

1. valuing the contribution of different individuals and communities
2. having some basic shared values and expectations
3. creating equal opportunities for people from different backgrounds
4. acting fairly in allocating resources or arbitrating between different interests
5. welcoming new arrivals while helping settled communities cope with change
6. building positive relationships between people from different backgrounds.

These characteristics are expressed positively as features that *should* be present. But they also imply action to tackle features that *shouldn't* be present – such as racism, anti-social behaviour or hostile media coverage.

This chapter will use these six elements as the headings to examine the part that housing organisations can play in creating cohesive communities. The chapter does not cover all the issues in detail. Where housing bodies have a key role – in creating mixed neighbourhoods, steering new investment, and developing and monitoring community cohesion strategies – these are dealt with in turn in the following chapters, and cross-references are made. Also, there are some aspects of cohesion work where housing organisations are unlikely to have a role – although, as we shall see from the examples, there are surprisingly few of these.

1. Valuing the contribution of different individuals and communities

Obviously, most neighbourhoods consist of a wide range of people of different ages, ethnic backgrounds and so on. Less obviously, this goes even for 'mono-cultural' areas, which often a have small ethnic minority population.

This aspect of community cohesion is about 'no one getting left out' – that communities work so as to include people rather than exclude them, and to ensure that everyone plays a role if the neighbourhood is changing. The converse would be if some people or groups within the neighbourhood felt rejected or even threatened. 'No one getting left out' applies not just to ethnic minorities – it applies to women as well as men, young as well as old.

This inclusiveness can only happen if there is some degree of 'self-knowledge' within the neighbourhood about who lives there, what kind of lives they lead, and what their views are about where they live and how they interact with other people. If people within the community are aware of each other, they can start to appreciate their different cultures and work together to achieve changes that might be needed in the neighbourhood. Housing organisations and the bodies they work with at neighbourhood level (tenants' and residents' groups) can help in this process in various ways.

Getting to know a neighbourhood

Where an area is undergoing major change, it is likely that resources will be available to housing organisations to work with and get to know communities in detail. There are many techniques for doing this. The Audit Commission has a useful *Knowing your Communities* toolkit which includes many appropriate methods.[31]

The CIH guide to *Community Engagement in Housing-Led Regeneration*[32] mentions informal approaches such as going along to established group meetings in an area

---

31   www.userfocus.audit-commission.gov.uk/
32   Lister, S *et al* (2007) *Community Engagement in Housing-Led Regeneration: A good practice guide*, chapter 5.

(eg parent and toddler groups) or talking to people in local shops and other community meeting points. These contacts should of course include finding and relating to BME communities, through refugee community organisations, places of worship (eg mosques and black-led churches) and events like festivals.

More formal methods (described in more detail in the CIH guide) include neighbourhood 'walkabouts' (eg with councillors or resident leaders) to look at and discuss local issues, door-to-door surveys and 'stakeholder interviews' with key local people, to find out their views about the area and encourage them to feel included in decision-making.

Developing local knowledge about an area is more difficult where little change is being instigated by the local authority or by the social landlord operating in the area. But even in these cases, changes may be occurring in who lives in the area or in the dynamics between different parts of the community. Little may be apparent to an outsider unless problems occur.

Housing organisations have information available to them which can give clues as to the state of community relations in an area. Social landlords will have monitoring data on their own stock, such as lettings and turnover. Landlords and their partners (eg in Crime and Disorder Reduction Partnerships – CDRPs) will have data on reported crime and ASB, including racist incidents. Some organisations have more sophisticated data-handling systems using GIS (geographical information systems) which enable them to combine and view the relationship between different data sets. Local authorities or social landlords may want to periodically test the level of community cohesion in an area, using special surveys. (Further methods of building up intelligence on communities and neighbourhoods are discussed in chapter 7.)

Here is an example of a landlord recognising and responding to neighbourhood change.

Tenant survey in Willow Park, Wythenshawe

Willow Park Housing Trust realised that the make-up of the 8,000 home Willow Park area was changing, so decided to carry out a full resident survey. They found that the ethnic composition of the area had changed markedly, with the BME population doubling (to 11%) in five years. Migrants had generally found the area friendly (although a proportion had experienced harassment); the main problem was lack of knowledge of local services or contact with service providers. Willow Park developed an action plan for the area, using the survey findings as a basis. Part of the plan is to develop more cross-community cultural events.

→

The work has now led to a wider partnership in Wythenshawe working on a community cohesion strategy for the area, and the housing trust has set up a residents' group to contribute to the strategy, aiming to ensure that it is 'owned' by the community as a whole.

More information: www.willow-park.co.uk

Tackling isolation

There are many examples of people getting 'left out' and their needs ignored. Some possible cases are:

- The difficulties and isolation experienced by elderly people in a neighbourhood, which may not be appreciated until major change takes place, eg demolition. It may then be difficult to meet their needs.

- New ethnic minority communities (eg refugees) moving into an area where there are different, long-standing BME communities; if this happens in private rented housing, local housing organisations may be unaware of the changes.

- Within established communities, some groups (eg Bangladeshi women) leading very isolated lives may have little contact outside their immediate circle and take no part in wider community activities.

The need to 'welcome' new arrivals in an area is dealt with later. Here we are concerned with established communities, and people or groups within them who suffer from isolation in different ways, including (as mentioned in the Commission report) the continued isolation of some second or third generation immigrants.

Why should housing organisations tackle isolation? Obviously, it is not the job even of a landlord to 'look after' everyone in an area. But, as mentioned in chapter 2, landlords do have 'ground level' knowledge which they can pass on to other agencies with a caring role, and they may want to take the lead themselves if the problems of isolation actually affect the overall functioning of an area – for example if disaffected young people in the neighbourhood are making the lives of other people a misery. Also, as part of their work with residents' and tenants' groups, they want to ensure that these bodies are as representative as possible and reach out to everyone in the area, not just (say) to white, middle-aged people.

Some examples of tackling different kinds of isolation are given opposite.

Examples of engaging with hard-to-reach groups within established communities

Group discussion sessions in Nelson, East Lancashire

As part of the work in Nelson for the housing market renewal pathfinder, Social Regeneration Consultants ran 15 group sessions covering about 300 people. Using participatory appraisal methods, informal discussions took place with groups including young people at a Connexions centre, older people at a luncheon club, women at Sure Start sessions and about 50 people from different BME organisations (attending focus group sessions). The different sessions showed the range of views about the area, and points of agreement, between different groups. A report was compiled detailing the views expressed, to feed into the plans for the area.

More information: sallythomas@socialregeneration.co.uk

West Midlands BME Women and Housing Forum

This multi-faith forum has provided a platform to enable Muslim women, among other BME women, to make a significant contribution to shaping housing policy in the West Midlands. The forum works with the Housing Corporation and local authorities. Ashram HA, a BME-led housing association, has played a leading role in establishing the network, which is now providing opportunities for Muslims to engage with debates about housing, environment and community cohesion.

Source: Ashram HA *Engaging Muslim Communities.*

'Images for Change' project, Walker

Walker is a traditional white, working class area of Newcastle, being regenerated through the Walker Riverside regeneration programme. 'Images for Change' involved giving members of the community disposable cameras to take photos expressing their views about the future of the area. The photographs were displayed at the local community centre and seen and discussed by about 600 residents.

In the second phase, residents were again given cameras and asked to interview six people across different residential, ethnic and generational boundaries. The purpose was to encourage people to embrace the transformation that Walker had gone through over the past few years, and to overcome fears associated with the changes. The project demonstrated that all groups need to be involved in planning as there was mistrust around the process of consultation.

Source: *Integration and Cohesion Case Studies*, p40.

Responding to tension within or between communities

The Commission's report points out that significant conflict between ethnic groups is relatively rare, although we should be aware that 'there are still chronic tensions bubbling under the surface of some local areas' (para. 6.41). The Commission points to the value of monitoring community tensions so that 'smaller rifts can be tackled before they become bigger ones'. This clearly makes sense and, even if housing organisations do not necessarily take the lead in this, they will want to be represented in any partnership approach.

Responding to tensions should (as, for example, would be the case with ASB) involve both preventative and, if still necessary, enforcement approaches. For example, in Waltham Forest there is an interagency approach to dealing with community tensions, given its significant Muslim community, which took preventative action when war was declared in Iraq. More recently, when ten local residents were arrested as part of an anti-terrorism operation a campaign was launched called 'Waltham Forest: 225,000 people, one community'.

The Commission suggests (para. 6.46) that there are three important elements to such work:

- All communities should be able to air their grievances and concerns, but for those discussions to have clear ground rules to deal (for example) with people saying things that might be taken as racist. It is important to give room for honest feelings to be aired, but for discussion to be managed by skilled mediators.
- It is more effective to meet people on their own territory initially – particularly young people. More lasting change is likely to be achieved if problems and issues are resolved in people's own context, surrounded by their peers.
- Local capacity should be used and built on. Local communities are resourceful: local knowledge, ideas about potential solutions, abilities and motivation reside within them. Tapping into this means that solutions are more likely to avoid damaging the bridges that exist, particularly those between communities and statutory agencies. This may mean understanding the skills of new migrants, and how they can act as community facilitators. Or more widely, recognising that local residents themselves can mediate if given support and training to do so.

In areas of recent migration, the Commission recommends that:

'...local authorities should ensure that existing homeowners, providers of affordable housing and the private rental sector are working together on a local strategy to tackle low-level community tensions and antisocial behaviour.' (para. 8.33)

Commissioned by the Metropolitan Police, the Institute for Community Cohesion has produced *A Practical Guide to Tension Monitoring for Local Authorities, Police Services and Partner Agencies*.[33] It recommends a partnership approach, involving local landlords,

---

33   Available at the ICoCo website (www.coventry.ac.uk/researchnet/d/361).

and also emphasises (and presents many examples of) preventative work at community level. Housing organisations should be aware and make use of the approaches in this guide: although rare, serious community conflict is often unexpected by those in authority. If followed, the steps recommended in the guide will make it easier to identify potential problems and take preventative action.

The report *Community Conflict: Causes and Action*[34] looks at examples of the main sources of conflict (eg inter-generational, racial and drugs-related) and includes a toolkit of approaches.

An example of *community mediation*, in this case following an earlier history of disturbances, is in Oldham and Burnley (an example which itself builds on experience of conflict resolution from Northern Ireland). (There is further material on and examples of community mediation at www.renewal.net).

Building Good Relations programme, Oldham and Burnley

Developed in partnership with Mediation Northern Ireland, the project develops awareness of and capacity to deliver mediation practice, as a tool for addressing community conflict. The project has worked at three levels:

- *Civic Leadership* – work with senior people in local agencies and elected politicians to develop their awareness of mediation practice and how it can be used as a tool to address communal conflict.
- *Practice Development* – training & mentoring of mediation practitioners and development of supportive structures for this process.
- *Work to address projects and cases* – the use of mediation to work through communal conflict and build good relations.

In Oldham, the project has been delivered since 2003. Starting with workshops with communities, it then focused on civic leadership and work in particular neighbourhoods. More recently, the project has trained local mediation practitioners, and has fed in lessons learned to the borough's tension monitoring systems. The ambition is now to provide conflict awareness and basic conflict resolution skills to a wide range of frontline staff and people in communities, as well as developing the existing practitioners as mediators capable of dealing with more difficult issues.

In Burnley, the work began in 2005 and has been funded by the housing market renewal pathfinder. It focused on four issues: housing market renewal, residential segregation, education and relationships between agencies and the communities they serve.

Source: *Our Shared Future*, para. 6.45.

---

34 Lemos, G (2004).

Another example, from Leicester, is from a place where no significant tensions were apparent but there was concern about the cultural isolation of certain communities in a multi-racial city.

Four Wards Intercultural Project, Leicester

The project brings together four culturally very different wards across Leicester: Belgrave (a mainly Hindu area); Spinney Hills (a largely Muslim area) and Braunstone and Saffron (two white working class areas). At the outset, a survey was carried out to gather baseline data to measure the extent of cultural integration in the city. The results suggested that the level of integration was less than anticipated.

Following this, a series of events were held, aimed at increasing exchange between the four wards. These included an exhibition in Belgrave challenging stereotypes of Pakistani women's place in the workforce; an evening of Asian music in a predominantly white area; an intercultural football tournament; a children's concert for schools across the four wards; and a Sikh play presented by a Muslim group to an audience drawn from all of the wards.

Bringing together the four wards has provided an arena for multicultural dialogue. The project tackles stereotypes and helps in 'myth busting'. By changing traditional channels of communication, new opportunities are provided for building sustainable relationships where they had not previously existed.

Source: *Integration and Cohesion Case Studies*, p178.

Tackling racist harassment and hate crime

If preventative measures fail, all housing organisations should, as part of their race equality work, have policies and practices in place to tackle racist harassment. This guide is not the place to review in detail the approaches that might be taken. There is the official publication *Tackling Racial Harassment: Code of Practice for Social Landlords*,[35] guidance from the CRE and resources such as www.raceactionnet.co.uk. Some of the more general guidance on tackling ASB and linked to the government's Respect agenda is also relevant.

Among other issues, local policies and practices should:

- have a clear definition of harassment, including examples that refer (for example) to new migrant groups and Gypsies and Travellers

---

35 Department of the Environment, Transport and the Regions, Housing Corporation and National Assembly for Wales (2001) *Tackling Racial Harassment: Code of Practice for Social Landlords* (available at www.communities.gov.uk/index.asp?id=1155712).

- put appropriate requirements into tenancy agreements, and get the support of tenants' groups for them
- ensure that hate crime is covered by the work of CDRPs (Coventry has a 'hate crime campaign' as an integral part of the city's CDRP)
- include comprehensive procedures on reporting incidents
- provide support for victims (including measures such as 24-hour panic alarms)
- provide positive support for groups such as newly-housed asylum seekers or other newcomers who might be more vulnerable
- have measures for dealing with perpetrators
- be based on effective and committed multi-agency working (housing, police, schools, etc)
- allow for monitoring so that new patterns of racist harassment (eg against new migrant groups) can be identified
- build in preventative measures.

Depending on the severity or pattern of incidents, it might be decided to adopt fresh approaches such as having a dedicated agency, creating special training programmes for staff involved, working directly with local schools, etc.

There is now also growing experience in imaginative ways of challenging and dealing with racist attitudes among young people.[36] More concentrated measures to deal with perpetrators – including restorative justice approaches (eg workshops with offenders) and/or anti-social behaviour orders – may also be needed.[37]

Tackling violent crime

Although outside the scope of this guide, in neighbourhoods where there is a significant problem of gun crime (or other violent crime) this can be a major source of tension, including tension between ethnic groups. Social landlords are likely to be part of strategies to tackle such crime through CDRPs, for example in having clear policies about how gun crime affects tenancies, in collaborating in witness protection schemes, and also in myth busting about such crime if fear within the community is disproportionate to the problem.

---

36 Some are cited in the *Integration and Cohesion Case Studies*. Also see numerous examples in Lemos, G (2005) *The Search for Tolerance – Challenging and changing racist attitudes among young people.* JRF, York.

37 The full range of methods of tackling ASB is discussed in Nixon, J and Hunter, C (2006) *Tackling Anti-Social Behaviour: Action Frameworks.* CIH for JRF. Community-based approaches are discussed, with examples, in Dearling, A *et al* (2006) *Supporting Safer Communities: Housing, crime and neighbourhoods.* CIH.

Social landlords may also be involved in community-based work to tackle the causes of such crime. An example is from Waltham Forest.

Waltham Forest – Defendin' Da Hood (DDH)

The London Borough of Waltham Forest and its partners developed a model for engaging with young people actively involved in, or on the periphery of, local gang culture, to reduce violence and gun crime and create ways to improve their life chances. Key partners include local housing associations.

Six events have been held so far, with young people enjoying entertainment and music, but always having to discuss a serious topic first – with the council and its partners committed to listening to what they say.

Following the July 7 bombings in London, the Council was asked by community leaders to organise an event to enable young Asian people to build better communications links with their elders. Other topics have included teenage pregnancy, gun crime, a missing teenager appeal, Christmas celebrations and community tolerance. There is now a large database of young people who have signed up to a text service, where the council sends information and alerts about events and other issues.

DDH has also resulted in the development of a radio station, and a group of young people have been trained to become a young people's independent advisory group. A play highlighting gun crime, 'Putting Respect Back onto the Streets', was written and performed by 14 young people.

The most dramatic outcome was a 40% reduction in violent crime around the time of the first event. A number of young people who attended the event are actively involved as partners in planning for the reduction of violent crime. Others are involved in planning a rolling programme of DDH meetings and events.

DDH is believed to be the largest ever consultation of excluded and vulnerable young people involved in gangs and ASB.

Further information: Michael.Jervis@walthamforest.gov.uk (also see www.lbwf.gov.uk/safety).

The Home Office 'Connected' website has a range of materials about dealing with gang culture and gun crime (see www.connected.gov.uk). It also has details of project funding under the 'Connected' programme, and information on more than 80 examples of projects in operation.

Building a shared vision for the area

If an area is to be subject to significant change (eg regeneration), then building a shared vision for it is both vital and, potentially, more readily achieved. There is considerable experience of ways of getting disparate communities to work together to build a shared vision. Several are mentioned in chapter 6 of the CIH guide to *Community Engagement in Housing-Led Regeneration*. Here is one from the Commission's work that particularly emphasises getting different groups to work constructively together. Later in the chapter we deal with the more common experience of building agreement around day-to-day issues in areas not subject to major change.

Holbeck Urban Village, Leeds

Holbeck is near to the homes of two of the 7/7 bombers, and regeneration of the area was being proposed in a sensitive local climate. There was local hesitancy in engaging with the outside world, and the city council was willing to commit more resources than usual to achieve meaningful and long-term consultation with local people.

A two day festival of high-profile events of community engagement launched a month long exhibition, 'What Kind of Place?', which encouraged debate about proposed changes. To overcome assumptions that the regeneration was aimed at attracting new business, rather than reviving the existing community, Multicultural Urban Design were appointed to engage intensively with both white working class and minority ethnic resident communities. This included presentations to women's groups and visits to mosques and churches.

The tense climate led to some apprehension from Muslim communities – one mosque refused entry to the engagement team and another expelled a team member who was distributing leaflets. The team therefore resorted to creative methods of overcoming 'community gatekeepers' to consult directly with people. This led to a procession of residents to attend the exhibition launch with other service providers, agencies and stakeholders, led by musicians. The consultation managed to engage sectors of the community beyond the 'usual suspects', developing a sense of ownership on the regeneration project. It strengthened community links in an anxious climate.

Source: *Integration and Cohesion Case Studies*, p49.

Tackling stigma and alienation

Part of the community cohesion challenge lies in dealing with the ways in which people see *themselves* and the area where they live, as well as in the ways they perceive other people or newcomers to an area. If an area has a bad reputation or people feel alienated from those in authority (the council, police, etc) these views may become compounded into group attitudes, whether in a neighbourhood as a whole, or (for example) among young people. This is a complex area, but some factors are important:[38]

- While a neighbourhood may have an 'identity', this can be a good as well as a bad thing. Identities tend to be comparative, so that some neighbourhoods may be stigmatised as 'bad', and residents may regard other neighbourhoods with hostility, especially if their own is physically isolated.

- Neighbourhoods may be labelled as 'black' or 'white' – even by people who live there – when in fact the reality is more complex.

- Alienation (low self-esteem, powerlessness, low expectations, etc) is strongly linked to people or groups being socially-excluded. This may in itself be at the root of hostility to others who are 'different'.

- Attitudes of young people are particularly important – they may pick up and magnify prevailing attitudes, and be more likely to act on them.

- Racism is a factor (eg in the towns where the 2001 disturbances occurred). Changing policies towards an area (eg ensuring fair direction of resources to different communities) may not be enough to change racist attitudes – other work may be needed.

- Attitudes are not just based on local circumstances but heavily influenced by the media (see chapter 8).

The way people or neighbourhoods perceive themselves can be a factor in tensions *between* geographically-separated communities. For example, while neighbourhoods in a town which have had internal conflicts in the past may now be more cohesive and integrated, hostility and the potential for conflict may still exist *between* neighbourhoods or communities (even those not near to each other).

One issue in dealing with this is ensuring fairness in distributing resources (dealt with later in this chapter and in chapter 5). Another can be the 'parallel lives' being led in different parts of the same town, and there are examples (eg from Leicester, above, and also from Bletchley, see page 59) of how to develop greater interaction. A further issue though is tackling basic alienation in an area and the reputation it has, challenging the 'them and us' attitudes which can prevail especially in poor, 'white' estates. One of the Leicester estates mentioned above provides an example of how doing this was combined with action to support newcomers moving into the area.

---

38 See Fitzpatrick, S (2004) *Poverty of Place* for background discussion of these arguments. Available from the 10 Downing Street website (www.pm.gov.uk/output/Page10025.asp).

Other measures which might be pursued include:

- Changing the names of areas with a poor reputation that are undergoing regeneration – in Birmingham, for example, the name 'Lee Bank' was changed to 'Attwood Green'.
- Promotion of the housing and the area facilities on offer – stressing the positive aspects) in for example the estate agent-style particulars used in some CBL schemes (see chapter 5).
- Myth busting – in this case, to counter misconceptions about the incidence of crime where these are inaccurate.

Braunstone Community Association, Leicester

Braunstone is a large, mainly social housing estate with over 5,000 households. Last census figures showed it to be 96% 'white'. Braunstone Community Association (BCA) runs a New Deal for Communities project whose aim is that within ten years it will be a 'beautiful place to live'.

Apart from major physical investment, significant community development work has aimed to change people's perceptions of Braunstone, both residents' and outsiders'. The proportion of residents who are satisfied with the area as a place to live has risen from 40% to 77% in five years. Work to give the estate a better reputation included staging the Leicester Comedy Festival, which attracted 3,000 people (many of whom would not previously have visited the area).

There has also been concentrated effort to make the estate safer for ethnic minority residents, because of pressing housing needs in the city generally. Despite considerable problems (and racist incidents), support work to individual families combined with coordinated action by the police to deal with any racist harassment have enabled more and more BME families to move there successfully – as an indication, one local school which had been largely white now has a much more ethnically-mixed intake.

More information: www.braunstone.com

---

2. Having some basic shared values and expectations

In discussing this element of cohesion, the Commission talks about 'key underlying values – such as fair play, tolerance and respect' (para. 5.11). It suggests that, where there are newcomers to an area such as new migrants, we should be looking for people to reach out to one another to some degree:

'What it might mean in practice is, rather than fostering resentment about the new people in the street who don't know when to put the bins out, others in the neighbourhood might ensure they have the right information from the local authority on when rubbish collection will be.' (para. 6.4)

The key aspects are that people have compatible ideas about what's important in the neighbourhood (eg tidy streets) and there are ways of resolving problems without them escalating or leading to long-running resentment.

There are many examples of apparently low key but (for local people) important problems being successfully dealt with in different areas (see three cases opposite).

These cases are one-off examples. Another approach is to work through 'estate agreements' or 'good neighbour agreements' to agree on ground rules and priorities across a whole estate or neighbourhood.[39] Croydon has taken this idea further to produce 'community action plans' for its estates.

Croydon's Community Action Plans

In estates where major investment is not planned, Croydon has a small community development team (including a youth involvement officer) which works with residents to agree on priorities for a particular estate, and the improved services and facilities that are needed. The team has a small budget of its own but relies on persuading other budget holders to cooperate in delivering the changes residents want. The action plans for each estate are developed in partnership with a 'forum' of local people and by holding 'planning days'.

Efforts are made to ensure that all groups within each estate take part, and activities are partly tailored to young people – for example on one estate young people took photographs to illustrate environmental problems they felt needed tackling.

The action plans have led to a range of improved facilities from multi-game ball courts to better lighting in estates. Overall, there has been a reduction in ASB and crime, and an improvement in resident satisfaction with their areas.

Source: http://beacons.idea.gov.uk/idk/aio/5060343

In older neighbourhoods where no major regeneration is planned, but there has been significant population change, it may be difficult to get the different communities to articulate their concerns. An example of a successful attempt to do this comes from Bolton (see page 56).

---

39   Examples are reviewed in CLG (2006) *Respect and Housing Management – Using good neighbour agreements*.

Action to tackle low key problems between communities

Community brokers: Acting together in Harrow

Residents in South Harrow contacted the council when groups of men began to gather at the end of one street for several hours a day. Some residents did not understand why the groups were there, and found them threatening.

Local police soon established that men were gathering in numbers to visit a nearby shop to purchase and chew Khat, a legal substance that can produce a temporary 'high'. This is a social pastime in Somalia, akin to drinking alcohol in the UK.

At first the shop denied the activity was going on, and progress was only made when the local Harrow Association of Somali Volunteer Organisations (HASVO) got involved, offering to act as mediators. The council and police set up a meeting with residents, Somali community representatives and local traders. Feedback later was that matters had improved and there was better understanding between the communities.

Source: www.rota.org.uk/pages/publications/briefings.htm

Northfields Estate, Leicester

The residents' association in Northfields have worked with the council to encourage refugees to be housed in the estate, and overcome local prejudices and fears about the changes taking place (see details on page 67).

One issue which arose was differences in attitudes towards day-to-day matters – an example was the habit of women from one new community of spitting in public, which older white residents found unpleasant. This proved easily dealt with; the association talked it over with women from the new community and they discussed it with neighbours. Soon the practice stopped.

Further information: northfieldscasp@btconnect.com

Northwards Housing Neighbourhood Warden Service

Northwards Housing (a North Manchester ALMO) has a warden service operating in an area experiencing an influx of EU migrant workers. They have made extensive efforts to engage with this new community, and have recruited a Polish-speaking female warden.

Their efforts have enabled them to tackle a number of issues that have arisen, such as problems between some families and local youths, late night parties occurring in some multi-occupied properties where migrant workers are living, and issues of under-age drinking (an older Polish man buying alcohol on behalf of local teenagers).

Further information: r.lawler@northwardshousing.co.uk

Bolton Community Drama

Hact (Housing Associations Charitable Trust) has a project – *Communities R Us* – which is promoting contact at neighbourhood level between different communities, focusing on areas where there has been recent migration. In Bolton, one aspect of the project has been a community-based drama.

The drama provided the catalyst for discussion, which may help to realise aspirations and resolve problems within the area. Painstaking door-to-door consultation provided material, with actors recruited from the neighbourhood, to 'play back' opinions about the area in a way which provoked discussion and helped to demonstrate that concerns are shared.

The drama was organised by a local person with experience in this field. The drama consisted of eight sketches. The actors were Somali, Indian Hindu, Muslim Asian and Kurdish. The sketches mainly relied on mime and were watched by over 100 people.

The audience clearly found it thought provoking and interesting. Discussion afterwards led to several positive comments about improving the area and to some active discussions between members of the three main resident groups (white, Asian and refugees). A follow up meeting has decided that it is a priority to hold more shared events.

More information about *Communities R Us*: www.hact.org.uk

3. Creating equal opportunities for people from different backgrounds

The Commission says that cohesion requires that 'those from different backgrounds have similar life opportunities, access to services and treatment' (para. 3.15). The interim report pointed out that in deprived areas, white people are particularly negative about how well people get on with each other. While deprived areas are not necessarily lacking in cohesion, deprivation characterises four out of the five sorts of area which the Commission includes in its 'typology' of areas that are *likely* to be less cohesive (para. 4.39). So, as a recent report on London says:[40]

'The hard graft of tackling disadvantage is therefore a fundamental driver of community cohesion.'

---

40   Muir, R (2007) *One London? – Change and cohesion in three London boroughs.* IPPR.

Again, tackling deprivation generally is too big an issue to cover in detail in the guide, but there are three broad measures which that are relevant:

- implementing the legal duty to promote equality that we discussed in chapter 2, so that people have equal access to services
- taking measures to improve people's access to welfare benefits and tackling 'financial exclusion'
- investing in training and other measures to increase skill levels and help people into jobs.

Within neighbourhoods, it is particularly important that community engagement or measures to improve or regenerate an area offer opportunities to all communities and do not widen further the 'gaps' which may exist between better-off and worse-off groups. One divisive factor may (for example) be a housing project which enables people who can afford to buy more modern properties to move into an area, but without consideration being given to providing opportunities that are accessible to existing residents.

Another element is that particular members of a community – young people, older people, women – are not given new opportunities because they do not take part in public meetings, or they otherwise get overlooked. Also, when one group within an area is markedly poorer than others, this can be a source of resentment from both sides. But as the Commission says, it is important to tackle inequalities for *all* groups – 'the underperformance of white working class boys at school just as much as the disproportionate disadvantage faced by Muslim groups' (para. 7.1). In situations where resources are limited, it is particularly important to be fair and transparent if hard choices have to be made between benefiting one group rather than another.

The rest of this section gives examples of creating equal opportunities for different groups or of tackling marked inequalities in a fair way.

Creating opportunities for young people

Social landlords are increasingly involved in creating opportunities for children and young people, particularly in deprived areas. Examples of housing-led work include:

- Tackling the issue of young people 'hanging around' in imaginative ways, eg projects to bring together young people and older people, or providing 'shelters' where young people can meet in an unsupervised way.
- Making land available or bidding for funds for ball courts, sports pitches and other facilities (see Croydon example above).

- Providing training opportunities for young people.

- Preventative work with ASB offenders or potential offenders (see Pathways2Progress, below).

- Resolving potential conflicts between groups in ways which also create opportunities for young people (see Bletchley example, below).

- Bringing young people into the decision-making processes on their area (see Croydon example above, and Nelson example, page 45).

All of these can also provide opportunities for strengthening community cohesion by also encouraging mixing between ethnic groups. The 'success factors' for work with young people are:[41]

- introducing people gradually, allowing trust to develop

- using a neutral setting

- providing interesting or skill-developing activities

- getting young people involved in managing the project

- targeting people who have the most negative attitudes

- aiming to create long-term initiatives

- involving schools.

Here are three housing-related examples.

Southampton's Junior Neighbourhood Wardens Scheme

This scheme actively engages children of 8-12 years old with Southampton's Neighbourhood Wardens and volunteers. The aim is to encourage children (particularly those on anti-social behaviour orders, acceptable behaviour contracts and young offenders) to divert from risky behaviours by taking an active role in local communities. Places are made available through direct contact with children (eg at schools, youth clubs, drop-ins and on the streets) or by referrals from partners. The scheme fosters better relations between inter-generational groups, by enabling children to carry out tasks for those of a different age group, who may be disabled or socially disadvantaged, thus improving mutual understanding.

Source: Commission report, para. 6.14.

---

41   Identified in background work for the Commission's research.

Pathways2Progress (P2P)

P2P provides tailored support to young people in Kensington and Chelsea who are at risk of crime and anti-social behaviour, or who have been in trouble with the law. For six years, Kensington Housing Trust's team of dedicated workers has been steering young people off the path of crime and disorder through one-to-one support and group activities. The project works by matching a young person with a volunteer mentor who can offer them one-to-one advice and practical help, and it aims to help young people develop and achieve positive and realistic goals for the future. In enabling them to find new interests, develop their skills, and fulfil their potential, P2P benefits its members, but also the wider community.

Source: www.chg.org.uk

'Round Ere, OO Cares?!' – Bletchley

Racially violent incidents had been occurring between young men from the Lakes Estate and the Bangladeshi community of Bletchley town centre. Street Dreams is a local organisation which aims to give young people a vehicle to voice their opinion. Initially, extensive consultation took place on the Lakes Estate, in the local school and in Bletchley, to plan the project and ensure access to all groups.

It was apparent that there were misunderstandings, ignorance and territorial problems. Services targeting young people had a 'patch' system of delivery – for example, the youth club in the town centre is only used by the Bangladeshi community and there is no club in the Lakes Estate. A 'Fun Day' was organised at the local secondary school by a group of young female volunteers. 150 people attended, from both areas. It was later discovered that some young people had come prepared for conflict (equipped with weapons); however, none occurred.

The project overcame barriers of residential segregation to encourage interaction between polarised communities. Sustained consultation with different communities ensured that the events were ones that people wanted. Five young people from the Lakes Estate and the Bangladeshi community have since become part of a new taskforce to ensure that the voice of young people is heard in decision-making in Bletchley.

Further information: info@street-dreams.org.uk

Provision made by housing organisations for young people should reflect fully the needs and aspirations of young people themselves. The CIH/LGA good practice guide on *Housing Strategies for Youth*[42] contains a reminder that involving young people

---

42   Folkard, K (1998), CIH and LGA.

from an early stage will help avoid under-used services, management difficulties and the need for major remodelling of projects.

Partnerships between social landlords and local schools can be particularly useful in leading to a coordinated strategy towards the needs of young people in an area.

Bringing older people into contact with other groups

As we pointed out above, a community cannot be cohesive if older people within it are isolated, and perhaps feel alienated by change taking place in the area. As with the examples of working with younger people, projects which give older people new opportunities can also be ways of bringing groups together who might not otherwise mix. For example, many of the networks which support asylum seekers in Glasgow depend partly on voluntary work by older people (eg through churches), who are also thereby brought into contact with new migrants. (In one centre there are shared facilities, eg computer classes.) Other possibilities are links between schools and sheltered schemes, or programmes where children befriend older people (and vice versa) to help bridge generation gaps. An example which bridges both cultural and generation gaps comes from Wales.

Charter HA's Learning Links

Learning Links, operating largely in the Pill area of Newport, brings together older residents with practical or language skills, and young people (such as asylum seekers) and other vulnerable groups. For example, an older resident who speaks Arabic and is keen on bike maintenance has been sharing his skills with young Iraqi asylum seekers. Other 'shared skills' have included passing the written part of driving tests, cooking, family budgeting and homemaking.

Learning Links is part of the EQUAL programme, funded by the European Social Fund, and won a UK Housing Award in 2004.

More details: www.charterhousing.co.uk and in *Inside Housing*, 12 November 2004.

Tackling the position of migrant groups who make little use of local services

New ethnic minority communities (refugees, migrant workers, etc) face barriers to accessing local services for various reasons – and as a result may miss out on opportunities or fail to make the contacts with other groups within the area. There are now many examples of housing-led projects or services to address this. This is one developed by two London housing associations.

'Reaching Out' in Enfield and Haringey

'Reaching Out' is part of an £87 million joint regeneration programme by London and Quadrant and Metropolitan Housing Trust in Edmonton Green, which delivered more than 700 new homes and refurbished a further 600. However, both HAs saw physical regeneration as only part of the task and set up 'Reaching Out' to work with the local Kurdish and Turkish communities, which account for 10% of the population and have difficulties gaining access to education, health care, housing and other services.

A Turkish outreach worker was appointed to address community concerns, made worse by language barriers. 'Reaching Out' offers a range of services, drop-in sessions and monthly information meetings on health, education, community safety and other issues. It publishes a quarterly newspaper, runs weekly English-language courses and supports a homework club with 118 young people. More than 200 people are involved in the project and nearly 1,000 have used its services.

Setting up a Kurdish and Turkish Residents' Association (KATRE), a registered charity, has ensured community ownership of project. Funding of more than £120,000 in cash and officer time has levered in a further £323,000 of grants.

The project won a Housing Corporation 2007 Gold Award for 'addressing the needs of diverse communities and harder to reach people and groups'.

Source: www.housingcorp.gov.uk/server/show/ConWebDoc.11225

Dealing with destitution and rough sleeping

If people within a community become destitute it is a serious problem both for them and any family or friends on whom they may depend, and can pose a problem for the wider community (eg reports from a Sheffield neighbourhood about destitute asylum seekers – young men – congregating in the area with no money and little to do). The reasons for destitution are varied. In the case of asylum seekers their applications may have been rejected but for various reasons they may not want or may not be able to return to their first country. Or they may have 'slipped through the net' of official support. There is now a small but growing problem (especially in London) of migrant workers, mainly from EU countries, becoming rough sleepers and (like rejected asylum seekers) having 'no recourse to public funds'.[43]

---

43   More information on destitution among asylum seekers is available through the *Opening Doors* project (training module 6: Destitution) and from the ICAR website (see Sources of Information at the end of the guide). The report by Homeless Link (2006) *A8 Nationals in London Homelessness Services* gives information on destitute migrant workers in London.

...d in their ability to assist destitute people because of
...unds' rule. There are many voluntary projects such as
...Action in Housing in Glasgow but the support they offer is
...tions are not prevented from helping destitute people, but
...ble for HB and may have no income to pay any rents or
...be best able to help in partnership with local agencies
...destitution but have limited resources. They may be able to
help by:

- Using charitable funds to assist drop-in or other local projects.
- Making premises available for use by other organisations.
- Working with local refugee or migrant organisations to support them in their work with destitute people.
- Engaging with local expertise/networks, eg legal advisers, local help and research projects.

So far, there appear to be few examples of housing organisations working directly in this area.

In the community cohesion context, it is important for housing organisations to be aware of and (as far as they can) ensure that destitution is tackled, especially where it is placing pressure on a community. There are already local studies in places such as Coventry, Leicester, Leeds and Newcastle showing the extent of destitution, the problems faced and lack of facilities.[44] By carrying out or sponsoring such studies, and using the results to build commitment to action, housing organisations may be able to coordinate better local provision and ameliorate the problems.

Assisting Gypsies and Travellers

As the Commission's report says:

> *'Discrimination against Gypsies and Travellers appears to be the last 'respectable'*
> *form of racism in Britain ... fuelled by the lack of suitable accommodation and a*
> *historic lack of recognition that Gypsies and Travellers are part of the local*
> *community. This has meant Gypsies and Travellers have had difficulties in accessing*
> *services and forming positive relationships with the communities in which they live.'*
> (para.7.8)

Antagonism towards Gypsies and Travellers can be a threat to community cohesion in some areas. An example of mediation between communities is given below. Social landlords need to bear in mind that Gypsies and Travellers increasingly seek and may be

---

44   Information on such studies is on the ICAR website (www.icar.org.uk/?lid=6571).

allocated social housing, and may then face problems of settling into a local area or of discrimination, in many of the same ways as newcomers from overseas.[45]

The Housing Act 2004 requires housing authorities to carry out accommodation needs assessments for Gypsies and Travellers. The quality of the approach to these is one of the issues considered by Audit Commission housing inspections. It is also likely that the CAA will consider how far LAAs/LSPs are undertaking their legal duty to promote good community relations, and provision for Gypsies and Travellers will be an aspect of this.

Resolving conflict between Gypsies and Travellers and the local community

Inadequate site provision for Gypsies and Travellers in an English county resulted in an unauthorised encampment. Tensions between the local community and Gypsies and Travellers led to an incident in which an effigy of a caravan with a gypsy family painted on the side was torched. The police subsequently arrested several people on suspicion of inciting racial hatred, and referred the case to the Crown Prosecution Service and the director of public prosecutions to consider prosecution under the Public Order Act.

Following the incident, external organisations with experience of similar situations were asked to get involved as mediators. A meeting was held for local authorities and community representatives. Following the meeting, an action plan was drawn up to help local authorities deal with potential conflict in the community. The local council agreed to improve its provision of services and sites for Gypsies and Travellers, and decided that it needed to increase involvement by all members of the community in its work and its consultations, including Gypsies and Travellers. The council reinstated its Gypsy and Traveller multi-agency forum, and employed a permanent liaison officer to work with Gypsies and Travellers in the area. Plans have been drawn up for permanent and transitory site provision across the county.

Source: www.catalystmagazine.org/duty/grr/general_case4.html.pr

---

4. Acting fairly in allocating resources or arbitrating between different interests

The Commission calls for 'a sense of equality and fairness for settled communities, just as much as positive action to close the gaps in outcomes for minority ethnic groups' (para. 7.3). It says that we need to respond to the sense of unfairness at a local level

---

45   Sources of guidance on these issues are the relevant section of the CRE website (www.cre.gov.uk/gdpract/g_and_t_facts.html); Richardson, J (2007) *Providing Gypsy and Traveller Sites: Contentious spaces*. CIH for JRF; and *Spaces and Places for Gypsies and Travellers: How planning can help* (www.pas.gov.uk/pas/core/page.do?pageId=37944).

that results from a feeling of competition for sometimes scarce resources, in five key ways (para. 7.12):

- *'by addressing the substantive issues being experienced by both majority and minority communities – whether levels of deprivation and under-achievement, or a wider lack of opportunity and therefore aspiration*
- *'by rebalancing communications to include all residents, not just particular target groups*
- *'by ensuring that local media understand the importance of their role in building integration and cohesion, and their responsibilities when reporting from within a context of diversity*
- *'by proactively tackling myths and misinformation circulating in local communities and causing division*
- *'by ensuring that all of this is scrutinised effectively by local scrutiny and risk structures, and is backed up by strong local data and intelligence.'*

These considerations influence all of the subsequent chapters of the guide. In this section we are particularly concerned with resource allocation to specific projects within neighbourhoods, and how fairness can be demonstrated and misconceptions dealt with. As the Commission says:

'...cohesion will depend on a trust in institutions to act fairly, to arbitrate fairly between different claims, and to allocate fairly resource across different communities.' (para. 3.14)

In the previous section of this chapter we made the case for targeting particular groups or particular kinds of need. But of course this carries the risk that other groups will feel left out. It is important that there is always an answer to the question 'why this group rather than another one?' There are some key principles in approaching this:

- *Get information* – about the area in general as well as the groups in question, so that the targeting can be justified, is based on demonstrable need, and is not arbitrary.
- *Create local partnerships* – work with, not in parallel to, the other agencies in the area, whether statutory, voluntary or community-based.
- *Involve the community* – decision-making at local level about what the priorities are, as long as the group involved is broadly-based, is more robust than a decision taken at the town hall (although some decisions *may* need to be taken centrally – see below).
- *Prepare the community* – if a particular group is to be targeted for good reason, but it might cause resentment, get the explanation in first.
- *Explain the wider benefits* – often the targeted investment will have some wider benefits. For example, providing kids with a kick-about area might mean they create fewer problems for older people.

- *Spread the benefits* – try to ensure that everyone in a neighbourhood gets some benefit from investment, even if it is partly concentrated on certain groups or parts of the area.
- *Be flexible* – if possible, keep resources for emerging needs and to respond to community views.
- *Don't ignore problems* – if resentment occurs, try to deal with it. In Burnley, the council organised visits so that people unfamiliar with high priority areas could see for themselves the problems being faced and better understand the council's decisions.
- *Bust myths* – later we discuss myth busting across a whole area or organisation, but it is equally important at local level. Make sure any resources or campaigns work at local level (eg in neighbourhood newspapers) as well as city wide.
- *Develop understanding* – people may have little idea of the problems which particular groups have, which means they are in greater need. It is important to make information available in ways that reach those who might otherwise criticise the priorities chosen.

Allied to this is the question of what the Commission called 'single group funding'. We give guidelines on this in appendix 1.

5. Welcoming new arrivals while helping settled communities cope with change

An overall strategy for community cohesion should have as a key element how to prepare for new arrivals to the area (or coming into a social landlord's stock). This will include aspects like allocating resources, briefing staff, etc. (Community cohesion strategies are dealt with in chapter 7.)

Here we are concerned with the process at neighbourhood level. Sometimes it will be possible to plan for change. A classic example of this is the areas where refugees have been accepted directly from refugee camps in Africa and Asia, through the 'Gateway' resettlement programme.[46] With careful explanation of their needs by the agencies concerned, local people have accepted and welcomed refugees through this programme in Sheffield, Bolton, Hull and elsewhere.

In many cases though, change will occur without local authorities or social landlords being aware in advance. The prime examples here are secondary migration of people accepted as refugees (who may drift away from the areas to which they were dispersed

---

[46] For more information on the programme see module 10 the *Opening Doors* training modules (www.cih.org/policy/openingdoors/).

as asylum seekers) and – especially recently – the arrival of migrant workers from EU accession states. In these cases there is a need for intelligence on what is happening (see chapter 7) and then for responses at local level which address the needs of the newcomers while respecting the feelings of the 'host' communities.

- *Providing information* to new arrivals to help them access services and adapt to life in their new neighbourhood.

- Where possible, *preparing existing communities* for the arrival of new groups. This involves explaining who, in general terms, the new arrivals will be and why the area has been chosen as an appropriate one for settlement. It is also important to provide information about the backgrounds to asylum seeker and refugee groups and why people find it necessary to seek asylum.

- *Engaging residents* in devising and providing solutions to meet the needs of the new groups. This could involve:
  - providing local information
  - local families acting as hosts
  - befriending schemes
  - efforts to bring the new communities into tenants' and residents' groups and community projects.

In some areas, where radical change is expected or there has been an unexpected and rapid influx of new people, a 'community support plan' may be needed, produced in consultation with local people and with the other agencies working in the area. If there are already locally-based migrant or refugee community organisations, it is vital to involve those too. Opposite are some examples of local approaches by housing organisations (see box).

More details on the elements of a 'community support plan' are in the CIH guide to *Housing and Support Services for Asylum Seekers and Refugees*, chapter 7. Further ideas on welcoming new migrants are in the *New European Migration* toolkit available from the IDeA website.[47]

6. Building positive relationships between people of different backgrounds

In many ways this whole chapter has been about this challenge, the final element of the Commission's definition of community cohesion. It is worth summarising though what the aims might be – and what they might not be – in trying to promote 'positive relationships', and what this means for housing organisations and other bodies working at neighbourhood level.

---

47   See www.idea.gov.uk/idk/core/page.do?pageId=6949778

A 'Warm Wulvern Welcome' for new migrants

Crewe and Nantwich has seen a recent influx of migrant workers – between 3,000 and 3,500 people. Wulvern Housing received an 'Invest to Save' grant to improve access to services for migrants, communication with existing communities and skill levels.

The project aims to develop/disseminate good practice, improve data collection on migrant communities, establish a multi-agency team and develop a contingency plan to cope with unforeseen change (eg in the local jobs market). Other elements include drop-in translation/advice sessions, ESOL classes, and building a relationship with employment agencies so that problems can be resolved.

More details: www.wulvernhousing.org.uk/

Southall Day Centre

Southall Day Centre in West London, provided by Catalyst Housing Group, offers a broad range of services to reduce residents' isolation, segregation, and social exclusion. It has helped many first generation migrants to settle, and provides ESOL, Fashion and Design, and IT training at the centre.

More details: www.chg.org.uk/

Local residents provide practical help for newcomers

Pennywell in Sunderland is an area which houses asylum seekers. Prior to their arrival Sunderland Housing briefed the residents' association, who were keen to help. One member, Gladys Chilton, decided to meet asylum seekers as they arrived, introduce them to neighbours, take them to shops and the post office – and challenge any negative reactions they encountered. She has been the coordinator for local social events which have been popular with long-term residents as well as newcomers. The reported result is that many asylum seekers now feel part of the local community.

More details: www.gentoosunderland.com/

A residents' association welcomes new migrants

Leicester City Council and local residents wanted to attract people to Northfields, a declining estate. They worked together on ideas about improving the estate and attracting newcomers. After 12 months preparatory work, closely involving the residents' association, groups of both asylum seekers and Somali migrants moved into the estate.

Meetings were held for people to voice any concerns, and people from new migrant communities in other parts of the city helped allay peoples' fears. Housing staff introduced new tenants to their neighbours on either side. Measures taken to improve the estate generally – for example by tackling ASB – were seen as benefiting all residents, not just newcomers.

More information: northfieldscasp@btconnect.com

The basics – people being civil to each other

First, there is tremendous importance in people simply being civil to each other as neighbours, in shops or when asking trivial questions such as what time it is. This is so basic that most of us are unaware of it – except of course when it is not there or a person or a group is uncivil to us. As the CIH evidence to the Commission put it (referring to the relevance of studies of mixed income neighbourhoods):

> '...tests of successful communities are not so much about there being strong relationships between people of different groups, but whether people generally feel comfortable with their neighbours, other parents at the school, etc, their children have friends, and they believe that the social mix of their neighbourhood contributes to the place being a good one. People tend to 'bump into' their neighbours, may to some extent cooperate on practical things but in most cases don't have deeper relationships. They regard neighbours in their area (even if of different tenure) as 'ordinary people' without making any special distinctions.'

In any particular neighbourhood, if this normal civility doesn't exist then that is both a problem in itself and may well be symptomatic of wider problems. Many of the examples in this chapter are ones where people in the neighbourhood came together in different ways, often with help from a social landlord, to establish or re-establish these normal relationships. Other important factors in day-to-day contact are the availability of spaces like parks, or of facilities like seats in shopping streets.

Why is there a need to go beyond this? – after all, one of the research papers for the Commission said that 'most people seem to be more than satisfied with maintaining cordial but distant relationships with their neighbours and particularly with strangers'.[48] Even if a large social landlord wanted to promote greater contact between residents than this suggests, it would be a big task to do it everywhere.

The main positive reason for wanting to achieve stronger relationships is that a neighbourhood is experiencing or is about to undergo change – for example, because new migrants are moving in, or because regeneration or redevelopment is to take place. Wider community engagement becomes necessary to face these changes.

The negative reason is in order for the community to face problems occurring in the area such as growing crime, or conflict between communities. Housing organisations have to prioritise, with residents, the neighbourhoods where cohesion is most at risk or where greater cohesion is important to their work and for the future of the neighbourhood. This all has to be part of a strategy towards community cohesion in the organisation's work – which we deal with in chapter 7.

---

48   Vertovec, S (2007) *New Complexities of Cohesion in Britain: Superdiversity, transnationalism and civil integration* (available at www.integrationandcohesion.org.uk).

Beyond the basics – bonding and bridging

In neighbourhoods where more active intervention is needed, as in many of the examples in this chapter, 'building positive relationships' has two elements (in addition to the 'basic civility' just described):

- *'Bonding'* – is about the sort of close relationships that exist within an extended family or between friends, which provide mutual support in day-to-day situations and help people cope with crises. People do of course draw this support from outside their neighbourhood – notably, some migrant groups. But in the case of poorer communities it often depends on local relationships. 'Bonding' is important but at the same time it can have some negative features – perhaps making communities very inward looking and defensive. This can sometimes happen both in 'white' estates and in 'traditional' areas of Asian settlement. An extreme example is a neighbourhood being dominated by gangs defending their 'patch'.

- *'Bridging'* – is about being part of wider networks that help people get jobs, influence authority and have wider experience outside their immediate circle or neighbourhood. Poor communities (both white and black) often lack these capacities, which would otherwise help them to change their circumstances. Helping them to 'bridge' can be a contributor to cohesion, providing of course that the 'bridging' involves bringing people together from different communities, not just reinforcing existing divisions within an area.

These two kinds of relationship within a neighbourhood are linked. 'Bridging' cannot happen if there is no 'bonding', but on the other hand too much 'bonding' may be an obstacle to change.

Fortunately, there are now many well-tested examples of communities working together to both 'bond' and 'bridge' – as we have seen in this chapter. They have all required some degree of community development or 'capacity building'.

Building community capacity

The Commission says that a key way of building more positive relationships is 'by encouraging and supporting people to become more active and empowered within their communities' (para.6.25). It points out that this is one of the main proposals of the 2006 local government white paper, but also says that a 'step change' is necessary in community empowerment.

In communities where these things are already happening, almost invariably there are some key individuals with the motivation and self-confidence to get things moving, and also the sensitivity to form the links needed to make sure that any group or activity is broadly-based. But, as the Commission says, 'these characteristics are not widespread' (para. 6.28).

There is therefore a need for much greater investment in community capacity building to develop people's skills, both individually and collectively, and to do so in ways which reflect diversity and build cohesion, as well as tackling any insularity and prejudice. Also any effective community development will involve programmes and activities that challenge low self-esteem, promote education and training opportunities, and engage with young people. One successful 'way in' to capacity building in deprived communities can be to focus on work with women in the area (eg the Turning Point Women's Centre in Braunstone, Leicester[49] – one of the new facilities in the example on page 53 – has had considerable success in developing the 'bridging' relationships just mentioned).

Community capacity building is defined by government as 'activities, resources and support that strengthen the skills, abilities and confidence of people and community groups to take effective action and leading roles in the development of their communities'.[50] In reality there is a spectrum of activities that might be called 'capacity building', from modest responses to requests from community groups (eg for a room for regular meetings), to much more ambitious aims of helping established groups deliver local services such as advice centres.

The CIH guide to *Community Engagement in Housing-Led Regeneration* has a chapter on community capacity building and the kinds of approaches that might be followed. The CIH guide to *Successful Neighbourhoods* has a chapter on devolving power to local level and the conditions for achieving this. Both guides have links to further resources on community development and capacity building.

The hact/NHF report *An Opportunity Waiting to Happen: Housing Associations as 'Community Anchors'* has numerous examples of how housing associations can build community capacity and act as support mechanisms for small community organisations.[51] This includes the example of Olmec, a subsidiary of the BME-led Presentation HA, which supports small community-based bodies. One of these is 'Black on Board' in Southwark, which trains people from BME communities to serve on HA boards or improve their prospects of working within HAs at senior levels.[52]

An example of capacity building linked specifically to cohesion comes from Bradford.

49   See http://beehive.thisisleicestershire.co.uk/default.asp?WCI=SiteHome&ID=2313&PageID=10398
50   Home Office (2004) *Firm Foundations*.
51   Wadhams, C (2006).
52   See www.olmec-ec.org.uk

Bradford Tenants' and Residents' Community Cohesion Project

The project, funded by a CLG Innovation into Action grant, enabled the tenants' organisation to appoint community cohesion workers on four estates. In each area the workers encouraged and helped create neighbourhood-based events and groups, focused on improving interaction between different communities in the areas. Their experiences led to an overall Area-Based Community Cohesion Plan, produced by tenants rather than by the social landlord. The story of the project was written up by residents as *How to Make a Community Cohesion Cake*.

Further information: www.innovationintoaction.org

Checklist on creating positive relationships

✓ What steps are being taken to identify and engage with hard-to-reach groups at neighbourhood level?

✓ How are tensions between communities identified and how are they dealt with?

✓ Are there mechanisms for engaging different groups living in estates, in planning improvements to their area?

✓ Are housing organisations actively involved in improving facilities for young people?

✓ What arrangements are there for identifying and welcoming new arrivals to an area such as refugees or migrants?

✓ Are there measures in place to help local communities develop their capacities in different ways?

CHAPTER 5

CREATING MORE MIXED NEIGHBOURHOODS

What this chapter is about:

- whether more mixed neighbourhoods are desirable
- opportunities for creating greater mix
- the role of housing organisations
- how to assess needs and balance demands
- housing choice and wider housing options
- moves to 'unfamiliar' areas and new housing 'pathways'
- poor conditions in the private sector
- neighbourhood management
- avoiding discrimination and monitoring results

Why more mixed neighbourhoods?

The Commission's interim report pointed out that it is easy to be simplistic about 'residential segregation' – that is, when minority communities cluster together in one (or just a few) neighbourhoods. For one thing, it may be partly a defensive reaction by people who feel safer if closer together, or may be a result as much of 'white flight' as minority groups themselves forming clusters. Those making submissions to the Commission (including CIH) pointed out that some minority clusters (eg Jewish people in Golders Green, or Leicester's 'Golden Mile' of Asian shops) are often commented on favourably. Also, white people often 'cluster' as much as ethnic minorities, and affluent people separate themselves from poor people in most cities.

Because the issue is not simple, and clustering may not be a problem anyway, only local appraisals (including asking local communities) can determine whether lack of mix is an issue. But there are several reasons why creating more mixed neighbourhoods, or at least opening up opportunities for mixing, might be desirable. Some are:

- *When 'clustering' limits people's housing choices or confines them to poor conditions* – see examples below.
- *When clustering promotes divisions between communities* – reinforcing hostile attitudes or racism, or reflecting alienation or stigma attached to living in certain places.
- *When new investment is taking place and all communities should benefit from it* – especially regeneration of an area, or development on greenfield sites which provide better housing or (for example) low-cost home ownership options.
- *When the use of other facilities, notably schools, is overwhelmingly influenced by catchment areas in which one ethnic group predominates.*

The case of housing choice being limited by clustering or segregation has several possible illustrations, such as:

- when a 'white' estate is unwelcoming to newcomers but has larger properties that should be accessible to all those in need
- when a mainly Asian area has mainly overcrowded, poor quality housing and people would welcome wider options if they felt secure about taking them
- when an inner city neighbourhood might be attractive to a range of people because of its proximity to city centre facilities, but it is seen as dominated by one ethnic group and therefore is unattractive.

However, any action to achieve greater mix in an established neighbourhood can damage community relations if imposed from above: it can only be successfully promoted through engagement with people in the area. Simply asking people whether segregation is an issue, however, may not work as their responses are likely to be conditioned by what they know and their possible fear of the unknown. (We suggest later some approaches such as discussing their housing needs and whether they might be more readily met by considering housing options elsewhere.)

The time needed to achieve change also needs to be born in mind – in most cases it will happen slowly, over a period of years. And other factors – such as tackling concentrations of poverty or addressing housing shortages – cannot be ignored if the more mixed community is also to be sustainable.

In new development areas, planning for mixed neighbourhoods needs to take place from the start – and making the new areas attractive to new residents from different ethnic communities must be built into the planning process, along with other aspects of 'sustainability' such as income and tenure mix.

The aim, however, is not to force people to mix; instead, it is about extending choices and creating new opportunities. Neither is the aim focused solely on people from black and minority ethnic communities. It is about all ethnic groups, and it is about having balanced communities in other ways, such as housing opportunities for young couples as well as for established households.

What opportunities are there for creating more mixed neighbourhoods?

The creation of more mixed neighbourhoods applies to new housing developments and to existing neighbourhoods. It is useful to look at the issue in three contexts:

'Brand new' neighbourhoods
Neighbourhoods created on large sites between existing settlements. Here it is possible to design balanced communities from the start. A substantial element of the south east growth areas in the CLG Sustainable Communities Plan will consist of such communities and it is essential that these areas be designed and developed with community cohesion principles firmly in mind, including the need for a range of housing types and tenures and for community infrastructure to support ethnically-mixed communities.

Existing neighbourhoods with opportunities for significant change
For example, those created through clearance and redevelopment. Many of the housing market renewal pathfinders and other regeneration areas provide examples of these kinds of areas.

Existing neighbourhoods with limited prospects of change
Places where there is a shortage of housing sites or where clearance of existing stock is unlikely. Here change needs to be brought about through altering the occupancy of the housing, possibly involving tenure change.

To make the material manageable, the first two types of opportunity, where physical change is possible through new development or regeneration, are considered separately in chapter 6. Change through management of existing neighbourhoods will be considered in this chapter. In practice, of course, across a town or city or across a landlord's stock, both sets of approaches are likely to be needed.

The role of housing organisations

The Commission argues that all affordable housing providers should have to demonstrate how their work is promoting community cohesion (para. 8.33). This means that it has to be taken into account as a criterion in the whole range of activities and services which they undertake. In delivering more 'mix' in existing neighbourhoods, the range of activities includes:

- *Assessing housing needs* – understanding people's housing aspirations and changing needs across an area, as a basis for responding through increases in supply or different ways of using the existing stock.
- *Balancing competing demands* – in a situation where, in most places, housing is in short supply, policies and practices must be scrupulously open and fair.
- *Improving choice in social housing* – having policies and practices which support people in making housing choices.
- *Widening the options that people consider* – additional options which enable people to improve their circumstances.
- *Supporting moves to unfamiliar areas* – encouraging and supporting moves to 'new' areas.
- *Providing additional housing 'pathways'* – creating further options within the existing housing stock.
- *Dealing with poor housing conditions* – especially where these affect community cohesion, or relate mainly to the housing circumstances of one community (eg migrant workers).
- *Promoting equal access* – tackling any barriers or false perceptions that might exist, that prevent people taking up opportunities for better housing.
- *Managing neighbourhoods* – in ways which promote community engagement and foster cohesion.
- *Developing targets and monitoring results* – from any of these measures.

These are the headings for the remainder of this chapter.

Assessing housing needs

Assessing housing need is a big subject on which considerable guidance is available. There is good practice guidance on assessing housing needs available from CLG[53] and on BME housing strategies from CIH.[54] Although dated, there is a useful guide to the assessment of black and minority ethnic housing needs, published by the Housing Corporation.[55] The main *community cohesion* aspects of assessing, understanding and responding to housing needs are:

- *Ensuring the needs of all communities are taken into account* – surveys may not show the different needs between apparently similar communities; or they may not include hard-to-reach groups; or they may be based on out-of-date data (eg 2001 census) when new migration has changed the profile of need.

---

53   Available at www.communities.gov.uk/index.asp?id=1155803
54   Blackaby, R and Chahal, H (2000) *Black and Minority Ethnic Housing Strategies: A good practice guide*. CIH.
55   See www.housingcorp.gov.uk/server/show/conWebDoc.1738

- *Understanding differences within communities* – for example, young couples setting up a home may have different aspirations from older, existing householders.

- *Finding out why different communities make more or less use of different options* – apart from the obvious example of ethnic minorities being under-represented in particular estates, it might be found that certain groups (eg refugees) are excessively represented in homelessness returns, suggesting that they are facing barriers to getting permanent housing.

- *Discussing different housing options* – the best needs surveys have qualitative elements, perhaps using more detailed survey work or focus groups, which throw light on the circumstances in which different groups might consider new or unfamiliar options or new areas, beyond the ones they initially prefer.

- *Having or developing a range of housing solutions* – the subtleties of needs or aspirations should influence how the organisation uses or adapts the existing housing stock, or seeks to increase the stock, to provide households with what are often called more attractive housing 'pathways'.

For a range of reasons, traditional 'needs surveys' which rely on questionnaires or market research approaches may not reveal the full picture. Consideration should be given to targeted work with particular groups, using methods which enable their concerns and aspirations to be expressed, and barriers in the way of their housing choices to be discussed.

Ways of doing this which also open up dialogue with under-represented groups are through focus groups and community-based surveys. Here are three innovative examples.

Assessing hidden housing needs in Bradford

After the disturbances of 2001, housing organisations in Bradford put considerable efforts into understanding different housing needs within the city and the obstacles people face in widening their housing choices. These included in-depth investigation of the housing aspirations of different communities, including for example looking at the aspirations of young Asian couples separately from those of older people. The report *Breaking Down the Barriers*[56] summarised the results of a number of different focus groups, which provided rich, qualitative material to 'flesh out' wider needs surveys.

---

56 Ratcliffe, P *et al* (2001). Published by CIH on behalf of Bradford MDC and others. The report is out of print but the methods used and the results are discussed in Harrison, M *et al* (2005) *Housing, 'Race' and Community Cohesion*. CIH.

Migrant group assesses own needs

Link Action is a group of Somali volunteers who worked with the Northern Refugee Centre to obtain training sponsored by Active Learning through Active Citizenship (www.togetherwecan.info/alac/). With the skills they developed they were able to carry out a survey into issues such as the problems faced by young Somali people, and produce a report *Somalis in Sheffield* directed at the local authority and other service providers, setting out the community's needs.

Further information: www.alacsy.org.uk

Census of the Gypsy and Traveller Community in Leeds

Leeds Racial Equality Council, supported by Leeds City Council, has used an innovative method of collecting data to quantify the numbers of Gypsies and Travellers. This assists the local authority to map their communities and improve services for these groups, facilitating greater integration into their locality. A census of Gypsies and Travellers living in the area captured basic information, including those living in caravans as well as a number of housed Gypsies and Travellers. The Gypsy and Traveller communities were consulted in the planning of the census to ensure that it was receptive to their needs. The census provided demographic data and revealed other issues relevant to integration and cohesion. It showed that living on unauthorised encampments was commonplace, with groups relocating regularly, creating tensions with resident communities and challenges for the Gypsy and Traveller community.

This clearly indicated a need for more sites in the area. The census also revealed that, in comparison to the wider population, the Gypsy and Traveller community has poor health levels, exacerbated by poor take-up of services. The evidence can be used to promote culturally-sensitive access to services and tackle barriers to integration.

Source: *Integration and Cohesion Case Studies*, p192.

An important way of getting qualitative information on needs (and barriers) is to engage with BME organisations. It is particularly important to ensure that contact is made with migrant or refugee community organisations, which exist in many cities (and sometimes smaller towns), offer important support to new community members but may not have developed relationships with the local authority or housing providers. Such contacts are considered further in chapter 8.

Assessing the housing needs of new migrant communities, such as migrant workers from EU countries, is particularly challenging because of lack of data, their heavy reliance on housing provided by employers or through the private rented sector, and the fact that many may be in the UK only for a short time. Local authorities in many areas have responded with their own surveys. Here is an example from a rural area.

Further examples are available from the joint hact/CIH project *Opening Doors*, from the toolkit on new migrants on the IDeA website and from the web resources on new migration based on the Audit Commission report *Crossing Borders* (details at the end of the guide in Sources of Information). Chapter 7 deals with the wider issues of population change and the demographic profile of areas, including new migration issues.

South Lincolnshire survey of migrant workers

South Holland DC, with other local partners, carried out a survey of over 600 migrant workers, as well as members of the indigenous community, which provided detailed information on housing and other needs, as well as their future plans, their attitudes towards the area and any problems they are having in integrating locally. Some 23% wanted to stay permanently and 33% said they hoped to bring their family to the UK. The study showed considerable exploitation in housing conditions, but with no major integration issues either from the viewpoint of the workers or of those surveyed in the indigenous community.

By building a picture of both the short-term problems the workers faced and their long-term intentions, the council has been able to begin to develop appropriate service responses.

Further information: dzaronaite@sholland.gov.uk

Balancing competing demands

In a situation where, in most places, housing is in short supply, trying to meet competing demands is both difficult and (often) done in the spotlight of political attention. The controversy over housing priorities in the London Borough of Barking and Dagenham, and the gains made by far right parties in its local elections, illustrate the dangers. A recent study of community cohesion in London produced these comments about new migrants from a focus group with white residents in the borough:[57]

---

57   Muir, R (2007) *One London? – Change and cohesion in three London Boroughs*. IPPR.

'They think it's great, they love it, they get off a lorry and are given everything...
money, a house, payouts.'

'When it comes down to the money, you see them and you're not going to get
money or a house. It puts me back one more step. I'm prejudiced before I even
know their story.'

According to the government's Citizenship Survey, 21 per cent of white respondents
feel that they would be treated worse by a local housing authority or a registered
social landlord than people of other races (compared with 13 per cent of BME
respondents). In other words, perceived discrimination is significantly higher among
white people.

Lack of affordable housing in many areas is a crucial driver of conflict, and resolving
the shortages is ultimately the only way to eliminate such misconceptions. Fairer
allocations and clearer communications about policies can only do so much: if families
are on a waiting list or transfer list, living in overcrowded conditions or in temporary
accommodation, they will be understandably frustrated and are likely to become
resentful of others.

Nevertheless, policies and practices *must* be scrupulously open and fair (and myths
tackled when they arise – see chapter 8). As the Commission says:

'There is a tension between the need to house people that have lived in an area a
long time (sometimes for generations) and those who have arrived more recently
and have particularly pressing social needs. There is also a potential for myths to
develop around who does and does not get allocated a home. Arbitrating between
these different needs involves difficult choices. In these circumstances it is essential
not only to be fair but also to be seen to be fair.' (para. 8.30)

The Commission recommends that local authorities should have 'community lettings
plans' that explicitly consider the dynamics of integration and cohesion locally, and
which apply to all providers in the area (para. 8.33).

At present, however, every authority has to have a publicly-available *Allocations*
Scheme, explaining its policy and how it operates. The current CLG guidance says this
about allocations and community cohesion:[58]

'Housing authorities should ensure that their allocation scheme and lettings plan are
representative of the community and promote community cohesion. In doing so,
they should ensure that the views of groups which are currently under-represented

---

58   CLG *Revision of the Code of Guidance on the Allocation of Accommodation*, para. 5.29 (available
      at http://comunities.gov.uk/index.asp?id=1152946).

in social housing are taken into account when consulting on their allocation scheme and developing their lettings plans. Housing authorities should also consider making realistic plans in respect of the allocation of accommodation to such groups, to monitor their lettings outcomes, and review their allocation practices where any group is shown to be disadvantaged.'

It goes on to say that authorities should consider ways to improve awareness of and access to social housing for BME households, and this is best done by adopting practices which are open and transparent and which give applicants a more active role in choosing their housing.

Allocations schemes can include a *local connections policy*, which would allow a degree of preference to be given to an applicant in need who has ties to an area (eg through family or work) as against someone who does not. Authorities could decide that a proportion of lettings would be made according to such criteria, provided that the main weighting was still on housing need.

Including such a provision might help to reduce the feeling that newly-arrived groups are getting an unfair share of lettings. However, the authority (or other provider following a similar policy) would have to be careful to ensure that such preference was not discriminatory. There is advice on this in the CRE *Code of Practice on Racial Equality in Housing*.[59]

At neighbourhood or estate level, social landlords can operate *local lettings policies*, but of course they cannot be used to discriminate in favour of an ethnic group (eg to achieve greater ethnic mix in an area). They can however be used to achieve social mix in other ways – for example, encouraging more young people into an area or (conversely) limiting further access by families with children into an area with few facilities for them. Such policies operate in parts of Plymouth and Gateshead. Some policies give greater preference to applicants who will make some contribution to the local community – Joseph Rowntree Housing Trust has such a scheme for people willing to commit to volunteer activities in its estates.[60]

It is also possible to apply a local connection criterion at estate level through a local lettings policy. For example, in Leeds, local lettings policies have been introduced to enable a customer, with a proven local connection, to be offered a property in preference to another customer with equivalent housing needs. Group lettings policies are also permissible that, on the basis of need, allow lettings to be grouped together

---

59   CRE (2006), p.22.
60   See the Trust website for details (www.jrht.org.uk/Policies/Community+lettings.htm).

(in both time and location) to make it easier (for example) for ethnic minority tenants to move to a particular estate (see page 87).

Housing providers also must ensure that if applicants are excluded from, or given lower priority in, allocations schemes, then this is on a fair basis. For example, they have the power to exclude or give reduced priority to individual applicants (but not types of applicant) on grounds of serious ASB. Also, while (as mentioned above) local connection can be taken into account in deciding priorities, applicants cannot actually be excluded from applying because (for example) they are non-resident in a particular area. Certain types of applicant are ineligible for local authority accommodation (or nominations) because they are subject to immigration control but, as emphasised in chapter 3, it is vitally important that providers are aware of the details of the law and that staff dealing with applicants are fully briefed.

As well as ensuring that policies are as fair as possible in local circumstances, housing providers should be open about the results of the policies (who receives the available housing) and publicise them. Most work on the public presentation of lettings schemes for social housing has been done in the context of choice-based lettings (CBL – see below). But of course the need for good publicity and explanation applies to any scheme. The challenge in situations like Barking and Dagenham is to publicise the outcomes of allocations policies in ways that really sink into people's consciousness and are widely seen as fair. This is much more difficult.

Here are two examples of well-publicised CBL schemes.

'B-with-us' – Blackburn with Darwen Council

This is a joint lettings scheme with a number of local agencies. Its attractive website (www.b-with-us.com/) has a good question and answer section in straightforward language. It includes information on recent lettings (although it does not summarise 'who gets what').

Sheffield 'Homefinder'

Sheffield's CBL scheme has a property shop accessed personally or through its web page (www.sheffieldpropertyshop.org.uk/). Results of lettings (which help to show the transparency of the scheme) are published weekly in a free local advertising newspaper. BME groups were involved in designing the scheme, and there is evidence of the satisfaction of BME customers with it.

Improving choice in social housing

The main way in which the government wants local authorities and social landlords to promote choice is through choice-based lettings (CBL). However, not all landlords operate such schemes, and other possibilities (and their implications for community cohesion) were set out in the CIH briefing paper *Offering Communities Real Choice – Lettings and Community Cohesion*.[61] Here we concentrate on CBL schemes as their use is growing rapidly, and promoting greater cohesion is often one driver for their adoption. Later we consider the other measures needed to complement CBL if schemes are to be fully effective.

The essential feature of CBL is that the customer moves from being a largely passive recipient of an offer to being an active 'member' of the scheme, making bids for available properties, which are advertised in various ways. Clearly this requires an input from the customer. People fluent in English and who are computer-literate are likely to manage much more easily than those who are not. Potential difficulties for members of minority groups include:[62]

- not understanding the system
- language problems
- not being computer literate
- not having ready access to a computer
- timing – bids are time critical
- poor knowledge of the wider area – needed to make informed choices
- unrealistic expectations – expecting to be successful quickly and being disappointed when this doesn't happen
- complexity of needs, eg requiring support or having other difficulties apart from lacking a house.

Most of these handicaps also apply equally to poor white communities. They can be overcome or reduced by good preparation for CBL. Possible steps include:

- contacting residents' and other community organisations (including those representing people who are relatively recent migrants, eg refugees)
- providing guidance or training to applicants either through such organisations or at local advice centres
- explaining the scheme in plain English and in minority languages
- allowing telephone bidding in the most commonly-spoken languages
- providing free computer facilities in different parts of the area
- training staff to assist vulnerable people or providing such a service through a community-based organisation.

61 Fotheringham, D and Perry, J (2003 – downloadable at www.cih.org/policy/CommunityCohesion.pdf).
62 Based on the Refugee Housing Association report (2005) *Reducing Barriers for Refugees Accessing Choice-Based Lettings Schemes*.

The CLG's main evaluation of CBL schemes has examples of community organisations in Sheffield, Newham and Bolton being involved in implementing CBL and giving assistance to community members, including refugees.[63]

In the case of refugee applicants, in a project run by Refugee Housing Association in Brent and Camden,[64] the main problem remained the obvious difficulty of actually getting attractive properties in the right location. This is largely a matter of supply, but measures can be taken (see below) to encourage people to widen their choices to areas they might not otherwise consider.

New migrants who are eligible for social housing may have particular difficulty because of lack of awareness of their eligibility.[65] Introducing a CBL scheme could be the occasion for wider publicity about the availability of, and access to, social housing. An example comes from Wakefield.

Contacting the Polish community in Wakefield

Wakefield's 'Homesearch' CBL scheme was introduced in February, 2007 with the aim of reaching as many people as possible – particularly the vulnerable or hard-to-reach. This includes more than 1,000 Polish people working in the area, hard-to-reach because they are scattered geographically. However, a Polish delicatessen was identified and contact made with it.

The delicatessen became a main point of contact with the Polish community:

- it was used to launch information sessions about CBL
- guidance/posters were produced in Polish (and cross-checked by the shop owners) for display in the shop
- a focus group was held with EU migrant workers.

Pre-launch information sessions on CBL were attended by over 1800 people and over 100 were Polish, indicating that the publicity had an effect.

Since the launch, more than 50 members of the Polish community have joined the CBL scheme and are actively taking part in bidding for properties.

Further information: pwood@wdh.co.uk

---

63 Pawson, H *et al* (2006) *Monitoring the Longer-Term Impact of Choice-Based Lettings*. CLG, chapter 6.

64 Refugee Housing Association (2005) – see above.

65 Under the Housing Act 1996, as amended in 2002, section 166 requires a housing authority to ensure that advice and information is available about the right to make an application and that assistance is available for those who are likely to have difficulty in making an application.

Widening the options that people consider

There has been concern that the impact of CBL might be to further encourage the 'clustering' of ethnic groups. However, the latest evaluation suggests that this is not the case.[66] There appears to be a general trend among BME communities across England towards greater dispersal, and CBL seems to be assisting that trend where it is in use. For example, following the introduction of CBL in Bradford (see below), there was a marked increased in lettings of social housing to Asian people – although this may of course be partly due to other measures which landlords have taken to increase the attractiveness of their housing.

Choice-based lettings has an impact in Bradford

Bradford Homehunter is a CBL scheme run by the LSVT organisation, Bradford Community Housing Trust (BCHT), as the managing agency for the local authority. The scheme offers applicants convenient, transparent and easy-to-follow processes when looking for rented homes with either BCHT or other local housing associations. It aims to ensure that BME applicants have the opportunity to move to all areas of the Bradford District, including those that have traditionally had a low BME population.

Significant successes so far include:

- Increase in lettings to BME households from 12.7% of the total in 2005/6 to 15.5% in 2006/7.
- Overall rise in BME membership of the scheme since it started in 2002, from 17% to 23% – there are now 10,521 registered BME bidders.
- Introduction of a new allocations policy to address changing demand for social housing and offer improved support for all vulnerable groups, including refugees and asylum seekers.
- A partnership with West Yorkshire Probation Service to give support to vulnerable ex-offenders and help provide security at neighbourhood level.

Bradford Homehunter's successful approach to increasing BME access to social housing has been recognised by housing partners. It has also been highlighted as an example of positive practice in the CRE *Code of Practice on Race Equality in Housing*.

Further information: Kathryn Wood, Homehunter Manager – 01274 254110.

---

66   Hawson (2006) – see above.

How can housing organisations further encourage people to widen the options they will consider? Social landlords should help people make more informed choices about their options – for example, if they consider 'unfamiliar' areas they might shorten their waiting time. They should use their computer systems to display the availability of dwellings of different types in different areas – applicants can then trade off perhaps a shorter wait for a home in an area that would not have been their first choice, with a longer wait for the first choice location. There is some evidence that people alter their bids to areas that were not their original preference in the light of information about supply and demand.

It is also good practice to maintain information on the facilities near to houses being advertised for letting – as might be the case with a sale advertised by an estate agent – ensuring that this includes information on (for example) nearby places of worship for different faith groups, shops, schools, community facilities, places of entertainment and public transport links. This can help overcome any unfamiliarity with the areas in which houses might become available.

Area preferences taken from application forms (or wider surveys) may reflect constrained choices – people can only name areas they have heard of and may well limit the stated preferences to those they would definitely live in rather than extend them to include those they may consider if the circumstances were right. Expanding opportunities involves social landlords proactively engaging people in discussion about area preferences, finding out what would be needed to make areas suitable and to 'market', in a sensitive way, the new opportunities that are being created.

As one practitioner commented for this guide:

> 'If choice is to be improved and housing needs met it is important for a housing organisation to not only understand housing aspirations. To truly build cohesive communities the organisation must understand the factors that influence housing choices. These may differ from area to area and between cultural groups. If top down integration is to be avoided then the right conditions need to be in place to encourage natural integration. This can only be achieved if those conditions are identified and understood. They are likely to be complex and the biggest barrier to successful integration. For example, recent research in Leicester shows that living near to a mosque is a very important factor affecting the housing choices of Muslims in the city.'

Of course, no-one wants to move to an area that is generally unpopular, has a bad reputation or offers a poor or even dangerous environment. Some areas may need significant investment *before* they are likely to be considered by anyone who does not already live there. Widening the options within the social rented stock cannot be separated from programmes to revive poor neighbourhoods or estates, including measures such as tackling ASB and addressing the 'Respect' agenda. It is worth bearing in mind that BME tenants of social housing are *more* likely to be dissatisfied with their housing and with their areas than white tenants.[67]

Supporting moves to unfamiliar areas

Several landlords now have arrangements for supporting new tenants moving to unfamiliar areas, especially those which might be unwelcoming to ethnic minority newcomers. The Leicester estates in chapter 4 (Braunstone, page 53 and Northfields page 67) and the Sheffield Homefinder scheme (this chapter, page 81) are cases where moves by BME tenants to unfamiliar areas have been supported and appear to have been successful. Further detailed examples are given in the CIH/Housing Corporation research study *How Housing Management can Contribute to Community Cohesion*.[68] An example from Oldham is given below.

First Choice Homes Oldham (FCHO) – Tenancy Support Service

First Choice Homes Oldham (an ALMO) has a dedicated team of equalities and community cohesion officers who offer housing support and advice to people who take up tenancies and also work with the local communities. One of these methods is through the Tenancy Support Service. It provides support to new and existing FCHO tenants who are moving into or are living in new communities. The service can help to:

- Identify needs and provide support from the time an applicant is offered a tenancy, for up to eight weeks after moving in (depending on their needs).
- Visit existing tenants to identify and support their needs.
- Organise and assist new tenants with practicalities of moving in, eg arranging utilities, removals, furniture, etc.
- Offer advice on welfare benefits, fill in forms, contact relevant agencies.
- Help develop links in the community.
- Act as a link person for other supporting agencies and services.
- Provide informal counselling and emotional support.
- Communicate in Bangla and Urdu.
- Provide an out-of-hours support service if needed.

The service has received a RaceActionNet award and has been highlighted as good practice by the Audit Commission.

Further information: Nimisha Misty (fcho.nimisha.mistry@oldham.gov.uk).

---

67 See Hills, J (2007) *Ends and Means – The future roles of social housing in England*. Centre for Analysis of Social Exclusion, p.75.
68 Robinson, D *et al* (2004).

These examples are of individual moves. Another option is to reserve a small proportion of properties for allocation according to specific needs, and/or to create 'group' lettings so households from a particular minority move to the same area at about the same time. Such lettings might have to be treated outside the normal lettings scheme (and CBL schemes often have provisions for such exceptions). An example might be allocating a proportion of three-bedroom houses on a large estate to larger families from outside the neighbourhood, in a context where larger accommodation is in short supply in other neighbourhoods. This might lead to several BME applicants being willing to move to an unfamiliar area, on the basis that they will not be 'alone' in making the move.

The ingredients in such schemes might include:

- identifying applicants who might need support or who have been encouraged to apply for unfamiliar areas
- if possible, linking these with other applicants from the same ethnic group who are willing to move to the same area (especially in moves to 'white' areas with few ethnic minority households)
- making accompanied visits to the areas/properties
- having information on nearby facilities such as places of worship or parent/toddler groups, etc
- giving practical assistance on tenancy sign up, such as help with utilities and registering with the GP and schools
- having access to interpreter services if necessary
- co-ordinating moves, including ensuring that repair/redecoration is done immediately before the tenant moves in
- liaising with neighbours and with the tenants' or residents' association to 'prepare the ground' and identify any possible problems
- liaising with police, if appropriate, and local support staff such as neighbourhood wardens
- introducing the new tenant to immediate neighbours on the day of the move
- making follow up visits to identify and deal with any problems.

In some cases, active protection by the team that deals with ASB or racial harassment might be needed.

Providing additional housing 'pathways'

Discussion so far in this chapter has concerned the existing social rented stock. Chapter 6 will consider new development – including small schemes specifically intended to open up opportunities in unfamiliar areas. There are, however, also possibilities for providing wider options within existing housing:

- *Common housing registers* or other measures for pooling properties between landlords so that applicants (eg in a CBL scheme) have a wider choice. The Locata scheme in West London and the Homefinder scheme in Devon and Cornwall are examples.

- *'Housing solutions' services* which offer a range of advice, and options in the private sector, for people who ask about available housing.

- *Guided referrals to private landlords* for applicants unlikely to be quickly eligible for social housing, eg Oxford's Home Choice scheme.

- *Self-help renovation of empty properties* such as the Canopy project in Leeds, aimed at refugees.[69]

- *Diversifying the stock* through, for example, making like-for-like sales and purchases.

- *Providing additional large properties by stock conversion* eg in a low demand area, converting adjacent semi-detached houses into one large house, suitable for a larger (possibly ethnic minority) family.

- *Options other than straightforward renting* such as low cost home ownership or the 'more varied menu' envisaged in the John Hills report on social housing and exemplified by the options provided to tenants by Notting Hill Housing.[70]

- *Alternative forms of finance* such as Sharia mortgages for potential Muslim house buyers.[71]

In part because of the Hills report, providing a 'more varied menu' for tenants and potential tenants, and creating more mixed-income communities within existing estates, are seen as key ways of making social housing more sustainable. In pursuing such wider options, including 'equity shares' and other ideas which cannot be considered here, it is important that social landlords adopt a 'community cohesion' test as well as whatever other criteria they are using to decide if they are viable. In other words, in addition to 'income mix', the objective in existing estates should also be 'social mix', including the widening of the housing opportunities of all ethnic groups and thus creating greater ethnic mix. We return to this issue in chapter 6 in considering new development and regeneration.

---

69   This and the previous example are among refugee housing solutions described in the CIH guide *Housing and Support Services for Asylum Seekers and Refugees* (Perry, J, 2005), chapter 4.

70   See Hills, J (2007) *Ends and Means – The future roles of social housing in England*. Centre for Analysis of Social Exclusion. Hills also mentions some of the other possibilities listed here.

71   Options are explained briefly on the 'Which' personal finance website (www.which-personal-finance-4u.co.uk:80/m_sharia_mortgages.htm). The growing availability of Sharia mortgages, which do not involve payment of interest (which is against the religious convictions of Muslims) from high street lenders, may improve the prospect of Muslim people taking up low cost home ownership opportunities away from areas of traditional settlement.

Dealing with poor housing conditions

Poor living conditions are obviously a barrier to achieving more mixed neighbourhoods (apart from their impact on existing residents). Fortunately, many of the issues of run-down housing in estates owned by social landlords have been addressed through the decent homes programme (although of course further investment may well be needed to make those estates really attractive places in which people will choose to live – especially people who do not live there already).

Community cohesion and achieving more mixed neighbourhoods is just as much an imperative in the private sector as in social housing, although of course the opportunities for intervention are different and often more limited. Major regeneration of older neighbourhoods, including new infill development, will be considered in chapter 6. Here we are concerned with conditions in older neighbourhoods where no significant new investment is planned (neighbourhood management is considered in the next section).

In many cases older, ethnically-mixed inner city neighbourhoods were the subject of intensive renewal programmes in the period until the early 1990s, but resources for such programmes are now severely reduced, although at the same time local authorities have much more discretion in how they use them. Outside declared Renewal Areas or areas covered by other programmes such as housing market renewal, the scope of action is now likely to be restricted to:

- Grant aid, possibly to the Decent Homes Standard – but on a restricted basis, and only in the most needy cases.
- Disabled Facilities Grants for making adaptations to private houses.
- Loan facilities towards home improvements.
- Assistance with repairs, home security or improvement work for older or disabled people through Home Improvement Agencies.
- Help with making houses more energy efficient.

For private rented housing, the available tools are:

- Enforcing the Housing Health and Safety Rating System and safety requirements (such as fire precautions).
- Mandatory licensing of Houses in Multiple Occupation (HMOs).
- Discretionary powers of additional licensing of HMOs.
- Selective licensing of general private rented sector properties.
- Management orders.
- Dealing with statutory overcrowding.
- Accreditation schemes for private landlords.

The tools for use in the private rented sector are described in the online guidance from CIH, CLG and IDeA *Ways and Means*.[72]

The purpose in briefly listing these tools is as a reminder that they are available, subject of course to resources also being available, and also to point out that it is important that measures for improving private sector conditions are non-discriminatory and help in achieving cohesive neighbourhoods. The Commission recommends (para. 8.33) that:

> *'Local authorities should be encouraged to identify areas that are experiencing particular issues that relate to integration and cohesion, and use fully the powers available to them to address these issues. These include powers on overcrowding, health and safety and environmental health, for example, as well as the ability to apply to the Communities Secretary for selective licensing for integration and cohesion reasons.*

> *'...They should take particular responsibility for ensuring landlords and tenants have the information they need to understand changes to the area and where practicable promote good landlord accreditation schemes.'*

As the Commission points out, poor conditions in the private rented sector, linked with overcrowding (which is three times more common for ethnic minority households), low level anti-social behaviour (eg noise at night time) and problems about keeping bins tidy and maintaining gardens can all cause tensions in neighbourhoods (as well as being unsatisfactory for the tenants affected).

This is particularly the case where the private rented property is occupied mainly by ethnic minority groups such as migrant workers. In many places, the growth in numbers of migrant workers has been absorbed by the private rented sector, with intensified use of existing properties, purchase of properties (sometimes pushing up prices in the neighbourhood) or even illegal use of attics, outbuildings, etc. In South Holland, for example, it is estimated that 59 per cent of migrant workers live in HMOs, with nearly 14 per cent sharing their accommodation with 7-10 others. In Breckland, the number of HMOs has grown from 40 to over 400 in four years.

An approach is needed which combines advice and encouragement with enforcement, working both with migrant workers themselves and with employers, agents and landlords. The proactive use of neighbourhood warden schemes can be very useful (see Northwards Housing example, page 55). In Herefordshire and Worcestershire, a survey of employers was used to begin to discuss housing issues and work jointly to tackle them. Two examples of partnership working come from the Audit Commission report *Crossing Borders*, which offers further guidance on this subject.[73]

---

72   Downloadable at www.cih.org/policy/WaysAndMeans.pdf
73   Audit Commission (2006).

Improving migrants' living conditions in Kerrier

Following local complaints, the local authority, police and other agencies combined to tackle a problem of illegal caravan sites housing migrant workers. Through discussion with the workers (using interpreters), and regular inspection visits, they have controlled the growth of sites and achieved better standards. Staff involved are now also part of the Migrant Worker Task Group of the Cornwall Strategic Partnership.

Responding to migration in Crewe and Nantwich

Around 3,000 migrant workers live in the borough, mainly in private rented housing. Complaints began to emerge about rubbish and noise problems in HMOs, and the council was concerned about the potential impact on community cohesion. It co-ordinated a response from a range of agencies, making links with the new community by using a Polish-speaking volunteer (who later became an employee). Mediation methods and community wardens were used to tackle neighbourhood environmental problems. (See also the Wulvern Housing example on page 67.)

Further information: *Crossing Borders*, case studies 1 and 2.

Southampton has a cross-agency strategy relating to new migrants (see page 121), and the action plan includes stronger use of licensing schemes.

Promoting equal access

In considering ways of widening housing choice and creating more mixed neighbourhoods, we should bear in mind that access to housing is mediated by many different agencies: landlords, vendors, estate and lettings agents and mortgage lenders. Intentionally or (more often) inadvertently, their practices can sometimes detract from cohesive neighbourhoods. There may be discriminatory practices, but more often they will consciously or unconsciously 'steer' people to or away from particular areas or properties. And other barriers might exist, or false perceptions on the part of customers, that prevent them taking up opportunities for better housing.

Discriminatory practices

Unlawful discrimination can be either direct or indirect and can operate in a way that denies access to housing to particular groups, either completely or in a way that restricts them to particular areas. Practices can vary from outright refusal to assist, through to numerous forms of indirect discrimination stemming from the operation of rules and requirements. It can also take more subtle forms, such as making untested assumptions about consumers' preferences or steering people towards, or away from, housing in particular areas.

Discriminatory practice may be unintentional. A particularly dangerous practice involves not passing on information about housing that is available in an area to an enquirer who is of a particular ethnic background because many of the people already living in that area are of a different ethnic background, on the assumption that the enquirer would not want to live there. Full use of advertising, including the use of the internet, allows customers to see what is available and will help to circumvent any attempts to 'steer' that may exist.

Mortgage lending policies can have an indirectly discriminatory effect. While there is no longer the 'redlining' of particular residential areas that existed up to three decades ago, mortgage lenders and those carrying out surveys for them need to be sure that they can justify any policy that treats whole classes of properties less favourably than others.

There are particular problems in low demand areas. Banks and building societies may be reluctant to lend because of fear of a fall in property prices, driving occupants to use fringe lenders offering less favourable terms. It remains important that their practices are not discriminatory on ethnic grounds.

Influencing household movements

Housing organisations can have a considerable influence on the mix of people living in an area. Estate agents and other property advisers may lead people to conclude that they should leave an area because 'it is going down hill' or 'prices are set to fall' or the 'wrong type of people are starting to move in'. Changes in the ethnic composition of an area will take place if this kind of advice is given to, and heeded by, people from one ethnic group more than another. For example, the 2001 Bradford study, *Breaking Down the Barriers*, reported:[74]

> '...damaging evidence of estate agents and property companies actively playing on racial fears to increase their "transaction" profits by generating rapid sales and "white flight"...If the street is mainly "white", estate agents notify residents of a potential fall in property values...The process of "block busting" was reported more than once during the consultation.'

---

74 Ratcliffe, P *et al* (2001), p82.

Other barriers and false perceptions

The most likely form of inadvertent discrimination is one that is much more difficult to identify – because it involves unconscious use of procedures or images that are off-putting to particular communities, or gives the impression that certain options are not available. A study of involvement of BME communities in stock transfer suggested three kinds of barriers that might exist – *basic, intermediate* and *difficult:*[75]

- *Basic barriers* – poor knowledge of the communities and inadequate efforts to communicate with them. Using an example from earlier in the chapter – refugees were not accessing a particular choice-based lettings scheme for various reasons, including unfamiliarity with computers and lack of fluency in English (see page 82). The *Opening Doors* project has also found widespread uncertainty among housing staff about the entitlements to housing of refugees and migrants.

- *Intermediate barriers* – issues about the organisation itself – people not trusting it, there being an unrepresentative workforce, it having the wrong public image. For example, the Bradford study quoted above also showed ignorance among BME communities about most housing associations in the area at that time (although not of Manningham HA, a prominent local BME-led association). Many studies of new migrants have shown ignorance of local housing services (or wrong assumptions that they are ineligible).

- *Difficult barriers* – arising from the minority communities themselves, for example that they are fragmented and difficult to contact, or there are 'minorities within minorities', such as women or young people, with whom it is difficult to communicate.

These problems may reflect lack of consciousness on the part of the organisations about the width of their customer base (or potential customer base). They could be rectified by wider contact with, and testing out of policies or publicity material on, the range of communities in their area; by careful monitoring of service usage and by measures to reach out to groups under-represented as customers. As part of meeting the obligation on social landlords to promote equality (see chapter 2), it is good practice for them to identify and seek to remove such barriers.

Possible action by local authorities

Bearing in mind their powers under the Local Government Act 2000 to promote the economic, social and environmental wellbeing of their area and their responsibilities as the strategic and enabling bodies, local authorities need to be concerned if there is evidence that housing organisations are creating segregated communities through direct discrimination or pressure or through the operation of rules or policies.

---

75   Centre for Urban and Regional Studies (2004) *Empowering communities, improving housing: Involving black and minority ethnic tenants and communities.* CLG, p3.

Where there appear to be problems, they have a number of avenues open to them:

- Conducting research to see how widespread the problem is.
- Engaging in dialogue. This could include:
  - discussion with specific organisations where alleged problems exist in order to seek a resolution;
  - more general discussions with agencies to warn of the possible dangers and to promote good practice – the use of existing consultative forums, for example private landlord forums and low demand pathfinder area forums, should be considered for this.
- Action under licensing schemes (for houses in multiple occupation or for other types of private rented properties in selected areas).
- By withholding support, for example not providing funding or land until the issues are resolved.
- Developing voluntary accreditation schemes for private landlords.
- Referral of the matter to the appropriate regulatory or professional body or to the Commission for Equality and Human Rights.

Managing neighbourhoods

Apart from their strategic relationship with community and resident groups (see chapter 8), social landlords may be involved in neighbourhood management initiatives at local level which also provide opportunities to pursue greater community cohesion. Again, it is outside the scope of this guide to discuss such initiatives in detail (a new CIH guide[76] to *Successful Neighbourhoods* does just that). However, many aspects of neighbourhood management are – as we have seen – relevant to community cohesion. Indeed, some of the areas where neighbourhood management has been adopted in some form are ethnically-mixed neighbourhoods or ones where greater social mix is being promoted. Because one of the main aims of neighbourhood management is to bring services closer to people, reflect local circumstances and create more community engagement, it can be an excellent vehicle for promoting community cohesion in existing neighbourhoods – the subject of this chapter.

Successful Neighbourhoods says that housing organisations can help to establish neighbourhood management in areas that might benefit from it if they:[77]

- take the lead in initiating discussions with the local authority and community organisations about establishing neighbourhood management
- work through LSPs and LAAs (see chapters 2 and 7)
- look for ways of funding neighbourhood management initiatives

---

76   Duncan, P and Thomas, S (2007). CIH.
77   *Successful Neighbourhoods*, pp 83-84.

- provide resources (eg seconded staff, local buildings)
- sponsor local tests of opinion about neighbourhood management
- broker arrangements with other housing providers (eg about rationalisation of stock management)
- begin to set up local services such as neighbourhood wardens
- consider transferring management of stock to a community-run body.

Here are two examples of housing-led neighbourhood management initiatives which have had a community cohesion focus.

Greater Dogsthorpe Partnership, Peterborough

In this housing-led partnership, a locally-based officer became the community's link point to all council services. The achievements so far have been:

- Perceived fairness of service delivery has increased, which reassures residents that their needs are being addressed – residents have channels of communication with service providers and feel that they are being listened to.
- Preventative measures – neighbourhood managers identify issues early and can respond to them rapidly so that tensions do not develop.
- Engagement, participation and civic pride – a neighbourhood partnership has been formed from local residents, ward councillors and service providers, which means that local residents are involved in how their area is being run and can contribute to decision making.
- Information sharing within the council has improved as a result – the neighbourhood manager within each neighbourhood shares knowledge with other services, and the dedicated team of staff ensures that all issues are dealt with quickly. This has improved effectiveness in service delivery and in responsiveness to changes in the neighbourhood.

Source: *What Works*, p147.

North Benwell Neighbourhood Management Partnership

This initiative in Newcastle-upon-Tyne was led by Home Group. It is aimed at stabilising and regenerating this ethnically-mixed area where there have been problems of empty properties, crime and a poor local environment. Eighteen people sit on the local Partnership Board, a mixture of residents and local agencies, chaired by a resident. It has taken on responsibility for delivering various local projects.

→

Successes include the BenFest community festival, which has created a positive image of a safe, well-run area, where house prices have stabilised despite its previous image. A neighbourhood warden team takes care of street scene issues; empty houses are painted so that they look occupied, and the physical appearance of streets does not suffer because of unoccupied properties.

Source: *Successful Neighbourhoods*, pp68 and 134-5.

Developing targets, collecting data and monitoring results

In the context of this chapter this means setting goals about aspects of cohesion at local level, such as encouraging wider housing choice, and assessing the impact on different communities and on creating more cohesive neighbourhoods. There is of course an obligation on social landlords to monitor their performance in many ways, including promotion of racial equality, and it is accepted practice to carry out an equalities impact assessment of (for example) allocations schemes, and any major changes to them. Detailed guidance on monitoring performance is available elsewhere (for example, in the CIH and Housing Corporation guide to *Black and Minority Ethnic Housing Strategies*).[78] Chapter 7 will cover wider community cohesion strategies and their monitoring.

This chapter has considered specific, neighbourhood-level interventions, and organisations need to know what their results are and whether they are working. To do this they can make use of their normal ethnic monitoring of their activities, providing that the categories they are using are sufficiently refined to accurately reflect the communities with which they work and recent changes such as new migration. So, for example, social landlords might want to set themselves outcome-based targets[79] to:

- Increase the proportion of ethnic minority tenants or residents in estates in which they are the main landlord (using a combination of lettings data and – in mixed neighbourhoods – information such as languages spoken in the local schools).

- Increase the proportion of ethnic minority applicants making bids under CBL schemes (eg 'raise the proportion of BME applicants from 10% to 20% within three years').

- Increase the proportion of ethnic minority applicants being allocated properties through CBL.

---

78 Blackaby, B and Chahal, K (2000).

79 Outcome-based targets are ones that aim for a measurable result, eg 'to increase the number of applicants from BME communities by ten per cent in the next year'. For more guidance on target-setting, see the toolkit *On Target: The practice of performance indicators* (available at www.audit-commission.gov.uk/performance/resource-publication.asp).

Other areas where monitoring performance may be important might include:

- Putting in place measures to encourage and assist ethnic minority applicants in making CBL bids, and monitor the results (as in the RHA project mentioned earlier).[80]

- Assessing the extent to which applicants through CBL match the profile of the population at large in the catchment area and/or the profile of those in housing need (if this information is known).

- In areas where specific measures are taken to assist the integration of new ethnic minority tenants, monitoring the success of the moves (eg interviewing new tenants after six months) and monitor incidents of and trends in racist harassment in the neighbourhood.

- If these areas are also low demand areas, and changing the ethnic mix is in part motivated by making better use of the stock and stabilising the area, monitoring void and turnover levels before and after the measures are taken, to judge their success.

- If other options apart from affordable rented housing are made available either to applicants or existing tenants, monitoring take up by ethnic group (to assess whether extra effort is needed to encourage take up by certain groups).

Of course, it is easy to set simplistic targets that do not necessarily indicate greater cohesion. Housing organisations may wish to consider what the most appropriate measures are jointly with other landlords in the area and/or partners in CBL schemes, and to consider the results both with tenant/resident groups and with BME community groups. The discussion in chapter 7 about local definitions of cohesion is also relevant.

Checklist on mixed neighbourhoods

✓ Have you considered whether action is needed to achieve greater mix in certain neighbourhoods?

✓ Is there an accurate assessment of current housing needs of all communities?

✓ What measures are being considered to widen housing choice?

✓ Are different housing 'pathways' being considered?

✓ Has there been consultation with local community organisations?

✓ Is there monitoring of the impact of lettings policies on different communities?

✓ Have any steps been taken to ensure hard-to-reach groups have access to the housing choices available?

---

80   Refugee Housing Association (2005) *Reducing Barriers for Refugees Accessing Choice-Based Lettings Schemes.*

CHAPTER 6

INVESTING FOR COHESIVE NEIGHBOURHOODS

What this chapter is about:

*   neighbourhood mix and the 'sustainability' agenda
*   ingredients in the 'mix'
*   creating opportunities through new development
*   creating opportunities through regeneration

Neighbourhood mix and sustainability

Neighbourhoods that are attractive, well-designed, which afford easy access to services and which meet all the criteria for sustainable communities are much more likely to be cohesive than those that are not sustainable. They are likely to be occupied by people who want to live there and who are not constantly seeking a way out. These kinds of neighbourhoods provide the right environment for interaction and mutual respect between those living there. This chapter looks at neighbourhoods where major change is to take place – through regeneration or new development – and the opportunities they present for promoting community cohesion.

Any policy about changing neighbourhoods needs to be set within wider aims about community sustainability. Government policy provides a good starting point. Several of the 'key requirements' for sustainable communities set out in the original Sustainable Communities Plan[81] are relevant to community cohesion. One has specific reference to it:

> *'a diverse, vibrant and creative local culture, encouraging pride in the community and cohesion within it'.*

Another calls for a physical mix of homes:

> *'a well-integrated mix of decent homes of different types and tenures to support a range of household sizes, ages and incomes'.*

The box shows one interpretation of the requirements for a sustainable community, based on the Sustainable Communities Plan but relating it to the neighbourhood agenda.

---

81   ODPM (2003) *Sustainable Communities: Building for the Future.*

SUCCESSFUL NEIGHBOURHOODS

The main ingredients

- A physically-integrated mix of housing tenures, offering a range of genuinely affordable options for people. Poor quality neighbourhoods with a high proportion of social renting and particularly private renting are less likely to be successful in the long term without significant tenure change and a more diverse mix of incomes.

- A range of adaptable house types and sizes, capable of meeting local community needs for the foreseeable future.

- A good quality, well-designed housing stock with regular, on-going investment in maintenance by both private owners and social landlords.

- A good quality, safe and well-maintained environment.

- Effective democratic neighbourhood representation.

- Active neighbourhood management, with direct involvement of the community in decision-making about local services and a commitment to joined-up operating by service providers.

- Community control of appropriate neighbourhood assets.

- A well-developed social network, with on-going investment in strengthening and widening social capital.

- A good degree of social cohesion between different communities living alongside each other.

- A clear sense of neighbourhood identity and belonging.

- Good access to essential community facilities for all age groups.

- Access to good schools and employment opportunities.

- Low levels of crime, drugs and anti-social behaviour, with visible and effective neighbourhood policing.

- A good, affordable public transport service, encouraging people to make some journeys without using their cars.

- Demonstrable, year-on-year improvements in the statistical indicators of deprivation – ill health, mortality, worklessness, illiteracy and school performance.

Source: reproduced from Duncan, P and Thomas, S (2007) *Successful Neighbourhoods – A good practice guide*. CIH.

However, the 'sustainability' agenda has been criticised for sometimes not including considerations of community cohesion. For example, the Sustainable Development Commission has commented that the Sustainable Communities Plan misses certain issues:[82]

> 'One is the concentration of seriously disadvantaged ethnic minorities in urban cores, and particularly in more deprived parts of major urban centres. There is a serious risk that the proposed growth areas in the South East will increase ethnic polarisation by drawing out better qualified, better connected households. The continued decline of low demand areas elsewhere in the country may have a similar racially and socially segregating effect. Both processes – of growth and decline – tend to concentrate more vulnerable and poorer communities within cities, particularly ethnic minorities.'

The Singh Commission has also called for integration and cohesion to be a firm part of the 'sustainable communities' agenda.

This chapter complements the previous one, which looked at communities not subject to major change. It considers what we called in the last chapter 'brand new neighbourhoods' created through new development, and also existing neighbourhoods undergoing significant change through regeneration and/or redevelopment. First, we look at what neighbourhood 'mix' means in different senses and how these can be brought together when making major investment in new development or regeneration.

What are the ingredients in the 'mix'?

The idea of achieving a mix of housing within neighbourhoods is a recurrent theme in government policy. For example, planning guidance[83] defines the objective of mixed neighbourhoods in terms of

> '...a variety of housing, particularly in terms of tenure and price and a mix of different households such as families with children, single person households and older people.'

Such guidance does not necessarily refer specifically to ethnic mix, but the Commission has said that integration and cohesion should be mainstreamed into local Sustainable Community Strategies and decisions on housing investment.

These are the different senses of 'mix' and how they relate to one another.

---

82   Sustainable Development Commission (2004) *Sustainable Communities and Sustainable Development – A review of the Sustainable Communities Plan*, p8.

83   CLG (2006) *Planning Policy Statement 3: Housing*.

Housing and tenure mix

Achieving an appropriate dwelling mix is important, not only because it can potentially affect the present social (including ethnic) mix of occupants, it can also have a longer-term effect on community cohesion. A variety of homes in terms of tenure, type, size and price expands the opportunities available for people to move home within their current area as their circumstances change – creating additional housing 'pathways' – in turn producing more sustainable and cohesive neighbourhoods.

One of the policy conclusions from a study of the long-established Birmingham suburb of Bournville is that:[84]

> '*A key development is providing pathways of housing choice that give people the opportunities to adjust their housing, without having to leave the neighbourhood. Irrespective of housing tenure or dwelling type, this would suggest that people could commit themselves to building networks and participating in activities.*'

Many areas fail to provide sufficient housing mix – for example, because they are mono-tenure, the houses are mainly of one size, or the housing types tend to exclude certain groups (eg single people or large families). A common problem is that houses are unaffordable or unavailable to newly-formed households who want to live close to their existing family in the area. A plan to achieve greater 'housing mix' needs to consider all these aspects in their local context.

Income and tenure mix

Related to housing and tenure mix is the aim of creating a greater mix of *incomes* and tenure, which is an element of government planning policy.[85] The goal here is to try to ensure that social housing tenants live in similar neighbourhoods to owner-occupiers, and that existing concentrations of social housing are gradually broken down so as to produce greater mix. A range of studies by the Joseph Rowntree Foundation (several published on their behalf by CIH) look at new and older mixed income communities, and there is a JRF good practice guide to *Creating and Sustaining Mixed Income Communities* (including a separate edition for Scotland). They point to a number of advantages of income/tenure mix, such as areas being more comfortable to live in and having a better image to outsiders. The Hills report encapsulated the advantages as:[86]

- avoiding stigmatisation
- avoiding potential declines in the quality of services (both private and public) in very low income areas

84 Groves, R *et al* (2003) *Neighbourhoods that Work: A study of the Bournville Estate, Birmingham*. The Policy Press, p50.

85 See *Planning Policy Statement 3*, mentioned above, p6.

86 Hills, J (2007), p179.

- having better protection of neighbourhood conditions
- providing links to economic activity for all those living in mixed areas
- more generally – 'avoiding part of society being cut off from the rest of it'.

While these policy aims must be borne in mind, in the context of community cohesion, having a strong mix of incomes in an area is perhaps less important than avoiding or tackling concentrations of poverty. Some of the reasons are:

- In very poor areas, social cohesion often breaks down, or may take a very inward-looking form which is hostile to newcomers and may exacerbate differences – such as ethnic differences.
- Poor, homogeneous communities (eg deprived, mono-ethnic estates) can develop a culture which is very hostile to outsiders, especially if they can be distinguished by race. This may be exacerbated by physical isolation – eg peripheral estates.
- There can be a breakdown of the normal social cohesion which inhibits crime and anti-social behaviour. Areas can reach 'tipping points' beyond which problems escalate.
- Where stigma is attached to living in an area, this exacerbates the problems (eg of getting jobs, or of low housing demand). Paradoxically, stigmatised areas sometimes have close-knit communities which want to continue living there – perhaps because of low expectations of being able to move.
- For ethnic minority groups living in poverty, conditions are made even worse by discrimination and racial inequality.
- Poverty can exacerbate tensions between minority ethnic groups in an area, who may be competing for resources such as community facilities.

Poverty and worklessness are therefore significant obstacles to community cohesion. As we said in chapter 4, it is beyond the scope of this guide to consider the methods that might be used to tackle them.[87] But measures of these kinds may well be needed in parallel with measures to create greater ethnic mix – if the overall outcome is to be more sustainable neighbourhoods.

Ethnic mix

Some of the areas where community cohesion might be a concern already have a significant ethnic mix – with long-standing white and BME communities, perhaps also with newer refugee or migrant communities (including migrants from recent EU accession states such as Poland). In mono-ethnic neighbourhoods, whether predominantly 'white' or predominantly of Asian or Black Caribbean origin, community

---

87   Further measures are discussed in Hills, pp187-191.

cohesion may seem a less obvious 'issue'. However, as we saw in the discussion of 'residential segregation' in chapter 5, existing mono-ethnic areas *can* be an obstacle to wider community cohesion across a town or city for various reasons, and the advantages of new housing developments should be available to *all* communities in an area.

Ethically-mixed communities therefore seem more likely to produce some of the conditions for wider community cohesion (such as valuing diversity and accepting cultural differences) than do areas lived in mainly by only one racial group, whether white or ethnic minority.

New development or regeneration schemes provide unparalleled opportunities for creating mixed communities, including ones which are ethnically-mixed. At the same time, if the principles of creating more sustainable communities are ignored, existing community divisions could be reinforced. Or the investment could be seen as favouring a particular community, causing resentment in other communities where no investment is taking place.

For these reasons, the Commission (and this guide) argue that major investment in creating more sustainable communities needs to include all the ingredients of 'mix', including providing the opportunity for ethnic mix wherever appropriate, as well as considering the impact of the investment on community cohesion in the area more generally. The rest of this chapter is about how to achieve this in (first) new development and (then) regeneration.

Creating opportunities through new development

The opportunities for promoting ethnic mix in new development

The government is committed to a significant increase in new house building, both public and private, and to major new developments, especially in the South East. As the Commission says (para. 8.30), this creates unique chances, which cannot be missed:

> 'Cohesive and integrated communities are more easily achieved where there is a mix of housing types and tenures, and where people are able to move between tenure types and between sizes of home as they move through life and face different personal demands. Government programmes to build new communities bring newcomers to communities and accelerate the pace of demographic change. Each new development is therefore an opportunity to build integration and cohesion – and this is writ large on a project such as the Thames Gateway, where 160,000 homes are projected to be built in an area that already has some cohesion challenges.'

Yet while contributing towards community cohesion has been considered in smaller, social housing developments, and in some larger, mixed-income developments in inner city areas, it has rarely formed part of the 'sustainability' agenda in larger developments outside inner cities or on greenfield sites, of the kind now being implemented.

Indeed, studies of mixed developments, or guides to future ones, can often miss the issues of ethnic mix and community cohesion. Chris Holmes, reviewing six wide-ranging reports on mixed-income developments conducted for the Joseph Rowntree Foundation,[88] said that one of the 'unanswered questions' in the studies was:

> *'How does ethnicity play out within these debates? In particular, how does the agenda of "mixed communities" sit alongside those of "community cohesion" and "community integration"?'*

Different approaches can be illustrated by three examples of different kinds of new development, two of which had a specific aim of promoting community cohesion and one which was based in an already ethnically-mixed area.

Creating culturally diverse communities in Bradford

Nashayman HA, working with Home HA, developed two housing schemes in Bradford in 2002 – in Allerton and in Westwood Park, neither of which were in traditional areas of settlement by Asian communities. One is about half a mile and the other three miles from the nearest settlement areas. Nashayman became involved in the developments as a new way of seeking to meet BME housing needs, as development opportunities are limited in traditional settlement areas.

Five years on, these two developments have become very popular both for BME and non-BME customers. Demand is very high and turnover has been very low. In Allerton, there have only been three vacancies during the five years and in Westwood Park only six vacancies.

Anecdotal evidence suggests that since the schemes were completed, people from BME backgrounds have gradually begun to move into the wider area, both through taking up tenancies with other landlords and through owner occupation.

Over the last five years, Nashayman has continued to develop schemes which are outside traditional BME areas in Bradford and the success of the above projects has been replicated.

Further information: ulfat.hussain@nashayman.org.uk

88   Holmes, C (2006) *Mixed Communities: Success and Sustainability*. JRF 'Foundations'.

Hulme, Manchester

Hulme is a well-known example of a large, inner city mixed development which is successful. About half the development is social renting and half is housing for sale. The blocks of different tenure are well-mixed. Planned as a socially-mixed development, with strong liaison with the communities in the area, the result has apparently been successful in terms of both ethnic mix and community cohesion. The social housing is representative (in terms of ethnic mix) of the local area; the private housing is less mixed but still reflects the make up of the population regionally. There is a reasonable proportion of professional people living in the area, even though many of the private sales were to previous tenants.

Residents' satisfaction is reasonably high, 24% said they were 'very satisfied' with the area in a recent study and some mentioned ethnic mix positively as a factor in this; some 23% were 'less than satisfied'. Those interviewed liked the sense of community and closeness to the city centre; the main concerns were about crime and drugs, and litter and vandalism.

Source: Silverman, E *et al* (2005) *A Good Place for Children? – Attracting and retaining families in inner urban mixed income communities.* CIH for JRF.

Angell Town, Brixton

Angell Town is the only purely social housing scheme to have been awarded a gold award by CABE. The project was driven by a residents' organisation, the Angell Town Community Project (ATCP), which was consulted throughout the design process by the architects they themselves had selected.

'People used to burn out their flats to get a transfer,' says Thomas Esterine, director of ATCP and a 40-year resident of the estate. 'There used to be that kind of desperation. But people want to live here now.'

Like other estates built in the 1970s (the original Angell Town estate was finished in 1976), Angell Town was characterised by inward-looking blocks. Mr Esterine says it was 'like an island'. ATCP decided to use five different designers to break away from the uniformity of the old estate. The architects agreed to hold regular resident surgeries, and input from these was incorporated into the finished design.

Involving the ethnically-diverse local population gave people a sense of pride, Mr Esterine says, that has translated into a better sense of community now the regeneration work has been completed. 'People make the best architects,' he says. 'We know the space that we live in.'

Source: *Inside Housing*, 22 June 2007.

Planning for ethnically-mixed communities

Broadly speaking, community cohesion principles can be taken into account in planning new developments in three ways, which are not mutually exclusive:

- Designing, promoting and letting or selling the scheme and the units in it, in ways that take account of the varied needs of, and will be attractive to, different communities.

- In mixed tenure/mixed income developments, considering the likely ethnic mix as part of the initial brief, setting aims of broadly reflecting the ethnic mix of the wider area across the tenures in the new development.

- Targeting a new development, or part of a development, at certain communities or groups, and ensuring that community cohesion principles are followed in planning it (eg that the new development will achieve more balanced provision in the area as a whole).

Setting aside for the moment the possibility of targeted developments, in the case of general new development which is based on government principles for achieving sustainable communities, the stages in the planning process where community cohesion might also be a consideration are:

- *Researching housing demand* – should include all the communities and potential markets in the catchment area for a project.

- *Community engagement* – the plans for the development could be discussed with ethnic minority community organisations and with nearby residents' associations, to enable their views to influence the brief.

- *Location* – if developments are remote from community-related facilities such as places of worship, shops, etc, their attractiveness to a range of ethnic groups will be more limited. Studies of the housing aspirations of different communities (see chapter 7) should obviously influence the brief for both the location and the content of the development.

- *Housing and tenure mix* – this could reflect known needs (eg from housing needs surveys or BME housing studies) for particular types of property. It is important not to make assumptions (eg that certain communities need large properties for extended families) as needs and aspirations are changing. Mixing tenures on the site (as opposed to separating them) is now regarded as good practice[89] and will help avoid any possibility of segregation of the development by income or ethnic group.

- *Safety and security* – are of course important for all communities but likely to be particularly so for people moving to an unfamiliar area. Principles of 'designing out crime' should be followed (see www.securedbydesign.com).

---

89   See Bailey, N et al (2006) *Creating and Sustaining Mixed Income Communities: A good practice guide.* CIH for JRF, chapter 3.

- *Layout* – this could reflect the needs for play areas or community facilities, attractive to all communities that might live in the new development, as well as features suggested in consultation with local community organisations. The continued importance of public spaces in promoting social interaction was confirmed in a recent study of Aylesbury.[90]

- *Meeting multiple needs* – designing homes to 'Lifetime Homes' principles will ensure that they can cater for a range of needs (bearing in mind that the percentage of disabled people is higher in poorer and in minority ethnic communities).

- *House design* – houses should be designed in ways which cater for different needs while still being attractive to all possible occupiers. The needs of different communities in relation to cooking, bathroom facilities, separate reception rooms, etc can often be met in unobtrusive ways (see sources of guidance below).

- *Advertising* – schemes could be advertised in ways that are likely to get the attention of different communities, and promotional staff could be representative of different communities in the area.

- *Letting of social housing* – this could reflect the principles discussed in chapter 5, which apply equally to newly-available properties as to the reletting of existing ones, including the possibility of support for ethnic minority tenants moving to unfamiliar areas.

- *Providing guidance* – to developers or (for example) those marketing low cost home ownership options on the ethnic mix of the community, which ideally should be reflected in who lives in the new development.

Unfortunately, there is little recent guidance on planning and designing new development to cater for different ethnic communities. The most comprehensive is the NHF's 1993 guide to *Accommodating Diversity: Housing design in a multicultural society*.[91] The Bridging NewcastleGateshead housing market renewal pathfinder has adapted this guidance and used other local studies to produce useful guidelines for the location and design of new developments, which also covers 'room by room' issues in the design of individual house types.[92]

The requirements listed above should be covered in the brief for the project, whether it is for a project directly commissioned by a housing association or local authority, or the brief is being prepared for council-owned land or as part of a section 106 agreement (under planning legislation). Nashayman HA, cited in the Bradford example above, have

---

90   Holland, C *et al* (2007) *Social Interactions in Urban Public Places*. JRF.
91   Oldfield King Planning Ltd (1993).
92   See *Promoting Equality and Sustainability through Housing Market Renewal* (downloadable at www.newcastlegatesheadpathfinder.co.uk).

since created a successful, ethnically-mixed development of rented and shared ownership properties in Calderdale, as a result of a section 106 agreement.

Of course, while the brief can reflect ethnic minority community needs, and set broad goals for community balance, it cannot determine what the outcome should be. Achieving greater social mix ultimately depends on the choices made by individual households.

Targeting developments

Developments specifically aimed at expanding the opportunities for ethnic minorities to move to unfamiliar areas, like the Bradford examples above, clearly require a different approach, which nevertheless must comply with race equality requirements. It normally means developing a scheme which is suitable for a range of people, but marketing it in ways that attract ethnic minority applicants as well as (say) existing nearby white communities. Ways in which this can be done include:

- Using a BME-led association to develop or manage the scheme, which is already familiar to and trusted by local BME communities.

- Aiming publicity at those BME communities where studies have shown there are housing needs that might be met through the new development.

- Offering applicants a letting within the scheme, who might have expressed a preference for traditional settlement areas, on the basis that the new housing meets their needs if not their preferred choice of area.

The rationale for targeting is usually one of the following:

- Provide additional housing options to solve problems of housing shortage or overcrowding in areas of traditional BME settlement.

- Meet demand for opportunities to move away from traditional settlement areas.

- Ensure that available land is used in ways which meet the most pressing needs (and this is done in ways which encourage people to take up the new opportunities).

- Ensure that new development earmarked for a site in a traditionally 'white' area fulfils a range of housing needs and doesn't cater only for (say) white households.

Careful thought needs to be given to the location of 'expanding opportunities' schemes. The new settlement areas will obviously have to be acceptable to people from minority communities and thorough consultations should be carried out before decisions are made. There may be 'no go' areas for some groups. The example schemes in this chapter are located a few miles from areas of traditional settlement – close enough for people to travel to visit relatives and to use specific facilities.

Survey work among Asian people in Bradford also suggests that likely locations for those leaving settlement areas were areas that were close by, although generally closeness to areas where many Asian people live was not the main reason why the areas were named. Instead, it was more to do with the quality of the houses than the areas themselves.[93]

The quality of housing management, and in particular the question of support to tenants in times of difficulty, is of central importance. The components of an effective support strategy are those outlined in chapter 5 (see page 86). A project in Leeds to integrate black and minority ethnic tenants in a new housing association development, away from traditional settlement areas, was evaluated independently and some conclusions were:[94]

- working closely with all newly-selected tenants is essential
- the needs and aspirations of *existing* communities, where the new housing is to be built, should also be an integral part of the project
- the image of incoming housing associations and the development needs careful promotion among existing residents
- nominations systems need to be agreed early on and should be flexible
- all the relevant agencies should be fully committed.

Identifying land and development opportunities for 'expanding opportunities' schemes is a matter for the local authority strategic and enabling role. A clear statement within the housing strategy statement that the authority intends to seek and give priority to suitable sites is a good starting point and will act as a spur to action by provider and funding agencies.

Creating opportunities through regeneration

Why community cohesion is important in regeneration

Regeneration projects offer the opportunity to renew the physical fabric of areas and also to create more sustainable communities. In considering the community cohesion dimension of regeneration, it is worth bearing in mind that:

- Regeneration often relates to diverse communities, where community cohesion is likely to be important.
- Decisions about investment, taken on the basis of need, may be perceived as favouring particular communities (eg inner city mainly BME communities or peripheral estates with mainly white communities)

93   Ratcliffe, P *et al* (2001).
94   Hawtin, M *et al* (1999) *Housing Integration and Resident Participation: Evaluation of a project to help BME tenants*. York Publishing Services for JRF.

- In some cases, regeneration may take place in areas with past or current community tensions or conflicts.

- Investing in the area is a massive opportunity, likely to lead to significant change – ignoring community cohesion requirements could prejudice the investment being made or lead to poor decision-making about the changes taking place.

- Community engagement should be integral to regeneration – and involving minority ethnic communities and hard-to-reach groups is likely to raise community cohesion issues.

The CIH guide to *Community Engagement in Housing-Led Regeneration* says:[95]

> *'Given that any regeneration programme is directed at deprived neighbourhoods, it will often include places where the combination of poverty and segregation creates the potential for community cohesion to break down or where issues already exist about how one group or community is perceived by another. On the positive side, action by agencies which results in improved community cohesion can count as a 'plus' for the programme.'*

This section of the chapter looks, first, at the different kinds of housing-led regeneration and the opportunities they provide and, second, at the stages in the process where community cohesion is an important consideration.

Different kinds of regeneration

There are a number of contexts in which regeneration strategies can assist in the creation of more mixed communities. The contexts considered here are tackling low demand, reconfiguring council estates and inner city regeneration.

1. Tackling low demand

Low demand can exist in a variety of different housing market contexts. Some areas are already ethnically-mixed but there are problems with sustainability, stock quality and the range of choices available. Other areas are less mixed and may well present opportunities for the creation of more diverse, and more sustainable, neighbourhoods. Tenure diversification may have a critical role to play both in boosting demand and in creating greater ethnic diversity. The answers will vary according to area depending on the needs and preferences of the different communities.

The housing market renewal pathfinder programme, operating in nine areas in England, provides a number of examples where community cohesion principles are being followed in designing and implementing major regeneration:[96]

---

95   CIH (2007).
96   There is more detail on these examples in the CIH guide *Community Engagement in Housing-Led Regeneration*.

- In Burnley, part of an ethnically-mixed and relatively cohesive neighbourhood is being redeveloped because of poor housing conditions. In making the rehousing plans, the council is trying to take into account as far as possible the existing social mix of the area and the desire of people to continue living near their neighbours.

- In Whitefield, Nelson, a process called 'Enquiry by Design'[97] was used to bring people in an ethnically-mixed neighbourhood together to decide on how to carry out partial redevelopment of the area. This inevitably involved the discussion of community cohesion, and how to strengthen it in the area through the regeneration process. The outcome was a masterplan which was endorsed in the final session of the 'Enquiry by Design' process.

- Also in Nelson, particular effort was made to engage hard-to-reach groups, including young people, older people and asylum seekers (see example on page 45).

- In Rochdale, the council has specialist 'property advisers' who work on a one-to-one basis with residents affected by redevelopment and rehousing plans. Their role is to 'hand-hold' during the process, ensuring residents are aware of the full range of choices available to them, signposting different options where necessary. The aim is to provide a culturally-sensitive service that ensures that no-one is disadvantaged by the redevelopment process and people are able, where at all possible, to improve their housing conditions.

2. Reconfiguring council estates

Although many housing providers are still focused on meeting the Decent Homes Standard, there is also wide awareness of the need to create more sustainable communities; this is one of the main areas of attention in the Hills report. Where wider regeneration of estates is taking place, it will often involve plans to reconfigure the housing stock through redevelopment, small-scale infill or remodelling of existing housing to provide different housing opportunities or 'pathways'.

The initial objective may be to better cater for existing needs in the area, but attention should focus not only on those needs but also on (a) needs and aspirations of those living elsewhere but which could be met there, and on (b) likely future need across the area. Regardless of the vehicle being used (retained management, a regeneration company, arms length management organisation [ALMO], stock transfer, etc), the appraisal of what is needed should take account of both the housing stock itself and the way the housing is managed.

For example, government guidance[98] stresses the need to cater for BME housing needs in any partial or whole stock transfer, and the resulting renovation or remodelling of

---

97   For more information see www.princes-foundation.org
98   See CLG (2004) *Housing Transfer Manual: 2005 programme*, paras. 4.29-4.33.

the housing stock. CIH and the Housing Corporation have also promoted the Community Gateway Model, which involves empowering local residents to take decisions about priorities for their areas, particularly in the context of stock transfer or establishing an ALMO.[99]

Questions that might be asked in considering how to reconfigure existing estates might include:

- Is the current housing stock capable of meeting the diverse needs of both the existing community and wider communities? If not, then what options are there to change it: through demolition and redevelopment, conversion, adaptation or acquisition?
- Would community cohesion objectives be easier to implement if ownership and management patterns were less monolithic and more diverse and is the way the housing is managed appropriate for diverse needs?
- Are there options such as: changes to the style of management, creating a new ethnic profile of the local staff, transfer of management to BME housing associations or involvement of BME associations in re-shaping the service?[100]

A particular challenge, frequently encountered even in ethnically-diverse local authority areas, is the traditional 'white' estate which has only a negligible BME population, and where there is both resistance to outsiders and lack of interest on behalf of BME communities in housing opportunities there, because of expected hostility. Approaches in this situation, considered earlier in the guide, include new development aimed at expanding opportunities for ethnic minorities (see the example from Nashayman HA, page 104) and encouraging more mixed use of the existing stock (see the Braunstone example from Leicester, page 53). Either does, of course, require considerable planning and consultation, as emphasised earlier.

3. Inner city regeneration

Major regeneration programmes in inner city areas could further enrich ethnic diversity, for example by providing new or refurbished middle range owner-occupied housing set in an improved environment. Imaginative ways of 're-packaging' traditional Victorian terraced housing have already been developed in the north of England (for example, the conversion by Urban Splash of 108 terraced units in Salford into 'upside down' houses, for which there was considerable demand). This kind of initiative could well be appropriate in other areas. Some authorities have responded to local demands for larger property by 'deconverting' large, multi-occupied Victorian houses to provide

---

99   For further information see the Community Gateway section of the CIH website (www.cih.org/gateway/).

100 For case studies of transfers, see Campbell Tickell (2005) *BME Housing Associations and Stock Transfers*. Housing Corporation.

larger family accommodation for sale or rent. (A point made earlier does however need to be borne in mind: it is important when creating options that might bring in new people also to consider better housing options for existing residents, or this can be a new source of tension.)

The combination of attractive housing near centres of employment, shopping and entertainment in city and town centres could for example be attractive to young middle class white or Indian households who may traditionally have thought only of more distant suburbs as places they would find acceptable.

An attempt to engage the existing community in a massive regeneration scheme, which will inevitably bring in (more affluent) newcomers, is King's Cross in London.

King's Cross Development Forum

The forum evolved from Camden Council's King's Cross team establishing a consultation process on the area's substantial regeneration project, including the mixed uses and affordable housing that would result from the development. The council sought to engage the local community in a long-term consultation that would include hard-to-reach groups, and run through from vision to actual building. The aim was to develop an inclusive and broad-based forum of residents and community groups that would inform, comment upon and respond to the challenges of the King's Cross development.

The development forum has been involved in each stage of the planning process and the consultation infrastructure has been strengthened through the council providing training for facilitators to meet with their communities and facilitate communication between the communities and the council. There has been good involvement by ethnic minority communities in the consultation. The forum has led to a wider public understanding of the planning system and it has had a real impact on the development proposals, which have changed significantly because of the work, reflecting successful community involvement in decision-making. The long-term consultation process has also challenged the pessimism that resulted from local residents' experience of 25 years of 'false starts' in the area's redevelopment.

Further information: Robert.west@camden.gov.uk

Earlier, in chapter 5, we considered the more limited renewal of older private housing and the opportunities which it provides (see page 89).

Stages in regeneration when community cohesion is important[101]

Almost every aspect of housing-led regeneration provides opportunities to improve community relations (and by the same token, to damage them if things go wrong). Key aspects include:

- understanding neighbourhoods
- community engagement and capacity building
- prioritising action between neighbourhoods
- rehousing
- improved management of neighbourhoods
- developing a strategic approach and monitoring outcomes.

These will be dealt with in turn.

1. Understanding neighbourhoods

Clearly, finding out about neighbourhoods means knowing who lives there, the needs they have and particular factors (like languages spoken in the area) which will have to be taken into account as engagement with the community develops. This work might reveal important changes in an area that were not previously known about: for example, recent migration through acceptance of asylum seekers (perhaps in private rented property), housing of refugees, or movement into the area of people looking for work, may all have changed the nature of the area and have implications for community relations. An example of finding out about community needs, and responding to them, comes from Gateshead.

Gateshead's Orthodox Jewish Community

Gateshead has a large Jewish community, particularly living in some of the neighbourhoods where work is taking place under HMR. Gateshead Council has a neighbourhood plan which identifies and responds to a range of needs expressed by the community. These include the need for larger houses in the area, which are now being provided through the HMR programme.

More information: the neighbourhood plan can be downloaded at www.gateshead.gov.uk/Building%20and%20Development/Regeneration/nplans.aspx

---

The government guidance on community cohesion in area-based initiatives suggests a range of issues that may arise at neighbourhood level.

---

101 This section of the guide draws mainly from material in chapter 10 of the CIH guide to *Community Engagement in Housing-Led Regeneration*.

Community cohesion and area-based initiatives –

Issues and suggested questions

- How well do different groups in the area get on?
- What are the main factors that prevent people from getting on? For example, is it a thematic issue such as housing or education, or a generational issue, or perhaps something related to the history of the area?
- Do people who have recently moved into the area take part in local activities?
- How long do people stay in the area?
- How well are people from different minority ethnic groups and, in particular, asylum seekers and refugees, accepted locally?
- How involved are younger, as well as older, people?
- How involved are women, compared to men?
- Are there certain people, for example those belonging to certain ethnic or faith groups, who do not take part in local activities to the same extent as others?
- Who is actively engaged in local activities?
- Is it mostly people from just one particular neighbourhood, or are local activities open to everyone who may be interested?
- How easy or difficult is it to find out about local activities?

Source: Home Office/ODPM (2004) *Building Community Cohesion into Area-Based Initiatives*.

Local surveys might include questions such as whether residents feel that their area is one where people from different backgrounds can get on well together (see further discussion of such surveys on page 130). Questions that provide useful indicators of community cohesion, especially if compared with other areas, also help in wider understanding of a neighbourhood.

2. Community engagement and capacity building

Community engagement in regeneration often involves considerable investment in building the capacity of communities, in part so that they can engage more effectively in the programme. It is also a longer-term investment in leaving sustainable networks and institutions in the area once regeneration has taken place.

This is an opportunity that applies in all neighbourhoods, but particularly those where major regeneration is taking place and resources might be available for building capacity in the communities concerned. Because of the changes that any regeneration programme is likely to bring about, different groups within the community can be encouraged (or may in any case take the opportunity) to have more contact with each other through residents' meetings and to 'join forces' to put their case to the agency carrying out the regeneration, in ways which may not have occurred before.

This issue was covered in more detail in chapter 4 (see page 69).

3. Prioritising action between neighbourhoods

One area of potential difficulty, in any programme which involves prioritising neighbourhoods, is the perception that an area which is primarily lived in by one ethnic group is being given preference over another, simply because of ethnic differences. If this problem arises, it should be tackled and not ignored. For example, if priority is based on deprivation or housing condition, facts can be publicised so that the basis of decision-making is clear.

In the housing market renewal pathfinder in Burnley, the local authority has worked in non-priority areas, including rural parishes, to explain the nature of the programme and deal with criticisms that particular areas are being favoured. It has even organised visits so that people unfamiliar with the high priority areas can see for themselves the problems being faced. In Nelson, the local authority has carried out less intensive action in some neighbourhoods to respond to potential criticisms that they are being ignored and other areas are being favoured.

4. Rehousing

In most regeneration schemes some rehousing is taking place because of demolition or to alleviate overcrowding. Whether rehousing is in purpose-built accommodation, or in the existing stock, it provides an opportunity both to meet the housing aspirations of the households concerned and to create more mixed communities. Research is likely to be carried out to find out the aspirations of those likely to move. In some cases there will be a strong desire to stay in the existing community, but in others people might aspire to change. While all residents will need support in making such moves, those from ethnic minorities moving to 'unfamiliar' areas may need the extra support mentioned in chapter 5 (see page 86).

5. Improved management of neighbourhoods

Improving the management of neighbourhoods enables problems to be tackled – such as vandalism and anti-social behaviour – which are often particular deterrents to their becoming more mixed. Tackling such problems also provides opportunities for people to work together in agreeing priorities, and even to work practically in clearing rubbish or tackling problem sites. This issue was also considered in chapter 5 (see page 94).

6. A strategic approach and monitoring outcomes

Community cohesion should be a factor in deciding courses of action and in monitoring the impact of regeneration. Agencies should be asking questions such as:

- will this help or hinder community cohesion?
- what will the impact be?
- should there be an overall strategy for community cohesion within the regeneration programme?
- do we have ways of measuring whether objectives are being met?

The changes being brought about by regeneration need to be seen against the background of wider work on community cohesion that is taking place in the area. Will regeneration contribute positively to that work? Are those taking the lead on community cohesion generally aware of and involved in the regeneration programme? Might the investment in particular areas bring charges of favouritism towards those areas? How will this be addressed? The actions which the regeneration agencies are taking provide an immense opportunity – but also a risk – in working towards community cohesion objectives.

Checklist on new development and regeneration

✓ Have all housing providers and enablers given active consideration to their role in creating more mixed neighbourhoods?

✓ Are proposals for expanding housing opportunities for black and minority ethnic communities being considered?

✓ Is there joint work between planning and housing officers on ways in which planning powers are being used to create more mixed neighbourhoods?

✓ Are new developments being promoted to all communities? Is their impact in terms of community cohesion being actively considered?

✓ Are all options being considered for the creation of more mixed neighbourhoods through regeneration programmes?

CHAPTER 7

COMMUNITY COHESION AND HOUSING STRATEGIES

What this chapter is about:

- housing as an element in community cohesion strategies
- responsibility for local strategies
- specific community cohesion and housing strategies
- elements of such a strategy and stages in its preparation

Housing as an element in community cohesion strategies

In chapter 2, we set out ten reasons why housing is important to community cohesion (summarised in the box below). We also described the policy and legislative background about cohesion and how it relates to housing. Most local authorities will need to have overall community cohesion strategies – or at the very least, follow the Commission's recommendations to consider community cohesion as a mainstream element in the local Sustainable Community Strategy. This chapter is not about how to draw up an overall strategy which covers all services. It is about (a) the strategic approach that could be taken by a *housing organisation* to its community cohesion work, and (b) the contribution this would make to a *wider* local strategy, its implementation and monitoring.

Why housing has a key role in community cohesion

1. Home and neighbourhood are key determinants in how people get on with each other

2. Housing investment is big investment – providing excellent opportunities to pursue community cohesion and mixed neighbourhoods

3. Housing is a scarce resource

→

4. Housing is the key component of neighbourhoods

5. Housing practitioners are 'close to the ground' – having the contacts and opportunities to engage with many communities and help them to be more cohesive

6. Cohesion is a vital element of 'sustainability' and 'place-shaping'

7. Housing is a 'way in' to promoting interaction between people

8. Housing can be the source of – but also the solution to – local conflicts

9. A major obstacle to integration is not knowing 'who lives where' – housing providers need this information and can be the source of it

10. Housing organisations are a key neighbourhood resource – their people, services and buildings can be vital in assisting wider community development

To set the context, the chapter considers first what the overall local strategy might look like, to which housing bodies might contribute. The rest of the chapter then looks in detail at the possible elements of a community cohesion and housing strategy.

Local community cohesion strategies

Community Cohesion: An action guide[102] sets out across-the-board guidance on how local authorities should seek to create greater community cohesion. The guidance states that local authorities should carry out a baseline assessment of how effectively their policies and programmes promote community cohesion in their districts. They may consider that their existing strategy documents (Sustainable Community Strategy, race equality scheme, crime and community safety strategy, neighbourhood renewal strategies, etc), perhaps with amendment, may be sufficient to address the relevant issues in their area. In many cases, however, they may decide that the issues are such that a specifically-focused community cohesion strategy, which complements the Sustainable Community Strategy, is needed.

The community cohesion agenda needs to permeate thinking at the highest levels. The need to create mixed neighbourhoods and to promote inter-community contact should be central to the thinking of Local Strategic Partnerships and should inform the preparation of Sustainable Community Strategies and strategies for neighbourhood regeneration and neighbourhood management. Option appraisals prior to major decisions, such as decisions about major regeneration or the possible transfer of local

---

102 Local Government Association (2004) *Community Cohesion: An action guide.* LGA (with the Home Office, ODPM, CRE, IDeA).

authority stock in an area, should include community cohesion as one of the criteria against which options are tested.

Strategies are not primarily about the production of a document. They are concerned with achieving change. Sustained change will only come about if sufficient numbers of people and agencies, especially those with the most power, are backing the strategy and are prepared to put resources into the programmes and initiatives that result.

Engaging the leading local agencies therefore is crucial to work on this issue. This involves asking questions such as:

- what is the local vision for community cohesion? – what should a cohesive city, town or village look like?
- what benefits does cohesion bring to neighbourhoods and to organisations?
- what are the risks if no action is taken to maintain or improve cohesion? – what tensions exist or might arise?
- how should each of the key players be involved in developing the strategy and in implementing the subsequent programmes?

Who has responsibility for developing a local community cohesion strategy will vary from place to place. The main possibilities are:

- *The Local Strategic Partnership (LSP)* – adopts community cohesion as a main theme, possibly to form a part of the *Sustainable Community Strategy*.
- *The local authority takes the lead* – through a central unit, such as the chief executive's policy team or equalities team.
- *Housing professionals take the lead* – some authorities will see the neighbourhood as the starting point, which gives a clear role for the housing service. The housing service may already have a BME housing strategy which could be the basis for a wider community cohesion strategy.
- *Where a strong lead is not being taken by the local authority* – housing associations could drive the agenda in particular cases (see below).

Problems in making progress will clearly exist where the local authority is not taking a sufficient lead. Where this is the case, housing associations, particularly larger ones, should consider carefully the need to take action. A two-pronged approach may be the most effective:

- In leading by example, by launching initiatives in neighbourhoods (eg multi-landlord estates) where they are significant stock holders.
- In lobbying for more strategic change, through housing consultative forums, through contact with councillors in areas where they have started to take their own initiatives and through their memberships of, or contacts on, strategic forums, such as LSPs and CDRPs.

Finally, community cohesion strategies have to link with other plans and strategies at local level. The Sustainable Community Strategy and the work of the LSP are the most important link, including Local Area Agreements and any regeneration programmes. Other links include the organisation's race equality scheme, and the authority's Local Development Framework (under planning legislation), its local housing strategy, and plans and budgets for community and youth work.

There are several examples of overall community cohesion strategies in section 15 of *Integration and Cohesion Case Studies* (eg Leicester, p208 and Bradford, p210). An interesting new approach to an overall strategy is provided by Southampton.

Southampton's 'New Communities Interagency Integration Strategy and Action Plan 2006-2010'

Southampton's strategy arises from the recognition of the importance of new migration in the city over the past few years, and attendant pressures on housing and on communities. It has four key themes, one of which is housing, and also prioritises contact with and support for migrant community organisations in the city. It also aims to include people whose immigration status is uncertain (eg asylum seekers whose cases have been rejected), recognising their impact on community cohesion.

The action plan covers several service areas, including housing; several of the action items are relevant to community development and/or community safety. It also has an element on information and publicity, covering issues such as the need to give accurate information to frontline staff, and to respond to hostile media stories.

The strategy recognises the need for partnership working and will be delivered through a multi-agency group. It also recognises the dynamic nature of the situation in the city and the need for regular review of the strategy.

Further information: anthony.pascoe@southampton.gov.uk

Designing a community cohesion and housing strategy

As with the preparation of any strategy, thought needs to be given to designing an appropriate *process*. Who should be involved in designing a community cohesion and housing strategy? Is there a need for new research or can existing data be re-worked? How does the housing strategy relate to the work of other service areas, such as planning and education? How can strategies be translated into action?

This section considers the process in the following stages:
- deciding on the scope of the strategy
- setting out the vision, aims and objectives
- deciding who needs to be involved and how
- understanding the local context
- main elements of a community cohesion and housing strategy
- implementing the strategy
- deploying resources
- publishing the strategy
- monitoring and evaluation.

Deciding on the scope of the strategy

Consideration should be given to the issues the strategy should cover. This guide focuses largely on differences based on ethnicity, but also gives examples of tackling possible tensions or conflict founded on other differences – for example, between old and young people in an area.

Community cohesion and housing strategies should concern housing in both private and social sectors.

The initial decision on scope may have to be re-visited after consultation has been carried out since engaging with people may raise issues that had not previously been considered.

Setting out the vision, aims and objectives

All strategies should contain a vision of what they are seeking to achieve. The guidance to local political leaders, *Leading Cohesive Communities*,[103] argues that they need to develop a 'compelling vision' for the type of place citizens want their locality to be. The vision should be created on a shared basis and political leaders should champion and defend it.

Housing-related aims and more precise objectives should flow from this shared vision. (Chapter 8 deals with the broader issue of getting political commitment to cohesion objectives.)

Deciding who needs to be involved and how

Decisions about the scope of the strategy will help shape discussions about who needs to be involved. 'Involvement' may mean simply being consulted and contributing ideas and information, through to being an active partner in preparing the strategy and in

103 IDeA/LGA (2006).

implementing the programme and initiatives that are finally agreed. (And it is important that the form and level of involvement are clear so that false expectations are not raised.)

The importance of partnership working cannot be over-stated. Most of the examples of good practice cited in this guide involve partnership working – many of the projects which appear to be succeeding in their objectives involve a wide range of partners from statutory, voluntary and community sectors.

Community Cohesion: An action guide recommends that an effective community cohesion strategy, underpinned by a shared vision, is vital for every area. It is essential that the local approach to cohesion is developed and owned by all local agencies (public, voluntary, community and private). LSPs may be the most appropriate vehicles for achieving this (if they have well-developed community involvement), but it might also be done (for example) as part of a regeneration programme.

Consultation should not be limited to the public, voluntary and community sectors. Efforts should be made to engage private sector agencies in issues that are relevant to them. While those in charge of local partnerships have a vital leadership role, ordinary people also need to be involved. One approach to involvement is that taken by the London Borough of Barking and Dagenham, which has faced considerable community cohesion challenges, often related to housing.

Barking and Dagenham – a local definition of cohesion

In Barking and Dagenham, the local authority, with its partners, has embarked on a programme of community engagement to develop a new community cohesion strategy for the borough. Part of that exercise is designed to develop a shared understanding of what a cohesive borough might look like. The following draft definition was developed for discussion as part of that process:

- *'a strong community who can expect equal and fair access to customer focused services; and*
- *a place where people, who through mutual respect can together enjoy safe and peaceful lives and look forward to the future.'*

Source: Commission report, para. 3.11.

Housing organisations should play their part in engaging ordinary people and community organisations. Consultation on community cohesion may be carried out in parallel with discussions on other issues, for example on the local housing strategy or the BME housing strategy. But all attempts must be made to ensure that consultation is thorough and inclusive, that proper account is taken of points that are made and feedback is given on the outcome. Forums used to consult on the strategy could also be involved in monitoring progress and holding council officers and others to account for action that should have been taken.

There are a number of issues that need to be discussed:

- why community cohesion is important
- the kinds of neighbourhoods that people want to live in
- findings and conclusions arising from the analysis of the local market and needs and preferences
- proposals – how programmes may need to be re-shaped to promote more mixed neighbourhoods
- the role that each organisation can play in delivering a community cohesion strategy.

Ways of getting community cohesion onto the local housing 'agenda'

- Input to Local Strategic Partnerships
- Crime and Disorder Reduction Partnerships
- Housing strategy conferences
- Housing needs surveys structured in ways that lead to greater understanding of different communities' needs
- Work with partner bodies – HAs, private landlords, voluntary organisations
- Consultation events on race equality issues
- Work with BME organisations, including migrant and refugee community organisations
- Community conferences
- Tenants' forums
- Articles in tenants' and community newsletters

Understanding the local context

Although emphasis is placed in *Community Cohesion: An action guide* on a corporate baseline assessment, it is important that local authorities and other social landlords develop a specific housing perspective on community cohesion. As part of their strategic housing role, local housing authorities are responsible for developing an understanding of the housing situation in their area across all tenures. The official guidance for English local authorities issued by CLG[104] states that, in addition to an up-to-date assessment of housing markets, the strategy should cover the 'role of housing in community cohesion' and the needs of particular sections of the community such as black and minority ethnic populations and those with particular support needs. Although there is good practice guidance on assessing housing needs (see chapter 5), there is no official guidance on the research that should underpin housing and community cohesion strategies.

In developing the knowledge base for the housing component of a community cohesion strategy, it is helpful to think about eight issues:

- local demography
- local housing markets
- how neighbourhoods work
- categorising neighbourhoods
- how cohesive neighbourhoods can be recognised
- measuring cohesion at neighbourhood level
- finding out about attitudes to housing and neighbourhoods
- the results of ethnic monitoring of service users.

These are now discussed in turn.

1. Local demography

Part of the analysis of the local context should involve an analysis of the ethnic composition of areas within a local authority's district. The Commission recommends (para. 4.24) that communities are mapped in each local area, and that the map is used as one way in which to identify tensions and opportunities.

As a first step, it is possible to map areas of concentration of particular ethnic communities using census information, although this is limited in use because simply mapping concentrations at a single point in time says nothing about changes taking place in different kinds of areas. Also, the census categories of ethnicity do not necessarily reflect the complexities of actual communities, and do not in any case enable asylum seekers and refugees to be recorded as such. Migration since the last census, especially from EU accession states, may have changed the picture completely in many areas.

Ways of developing a more detailed picture of local demography and how it is changing include:

- *Migration – overall picture* – analysis of available data from the worker registration scheme or from requests for National Insurance numbers (see box overleaf).

---

104 See www.communities.gov.uk/index.asp?id=1503206

- *Migration – integration issues* – Various studies by local authorities or housing associations have used their own local surveys either of migrant workers or employers, or both. An example of a local survey in South Lincolnshire was given in chapter 5 (see page 78) and a special survey was used in the Southampton strategy mentioned earlier in this chapter.

- *Specific studies of ethnic minority communities* – such as the Bradford study *Breaking Down the Barriers* (see page 76) or the study of Gypsy and Traveller communities in Leeds (see page 77).

- *Engaging with groups from new migrant communities* – for example, some refugee community organisations have carried out local surveys (see page 77), or might be able to do so, or may be willing to share their own data on needs (eg from their own advice sessions).

Limitations of national data on new migrants and sources of guidance on local surveys

There are significant problems with establishing numbers and characteristics of new migrants at local/regional level using disaggregated national data. These include:

- Worker registration data (available at www.ind.homeoffice.gov.uk/aboutus/reports/accession_monitoring_report) only record initial registrations – there is no requirement to 'deregister' and also little incentive to re-register when changing jobs. Some data appear by the employer's address – presumably in cases where accommodation is provided in advance. The requirement to register only covers a proportion of new migrants.

- National Insurance (NI) registration data for local areas are very useful (see www.dwp.gov.uk/asd/asd1/niall/nino_allocation.asp) but NI is not always applied for immediately so the data under-represent actual numbers.

- Census data are out-of-date and appear to under-represent migrants.

Available central data are therefore useful to provide a 'snapshot' but may significantly underestimate migrant populations, especially in areas of high turnover.

Many organisations have therefore supplemented data from these sources with local surveys. While there is no central guidance on doing such surveys, there are good practice points and examples available: for example, the *Opening Doors* project has a review of 16 local and regional studies, the IDeA has produced a toolkit *New European Migration* and the Audit Commission has published *Crossing Borders* together with guidance on its website about use of the data sources mentioned here (see Sources of Information at the end of the guide for details).

2. Local housing markets

There may be changes in the local housing market that affect the composition of communities, particularly in relation to house prices, rents and incomes. These factors have an impact on the affordability of housing in different areas and are therefore crucial for the way in which different groups can access housing. Competition (or perceived competition) in the local housing market is a potential source of tension. For example:

- As we emphasised in chapter 5, lettings policies for social housing not only determine who gains access to it but may be under intense scrutiny locally, with people feeling discriminated against when in reality policies are fair.

- Different communities have different attitudes towards the market. For example, in Leicester monitoring of lettings show that Black Africans are the second biggest ethnic group in many parts of the city, including mainly white areas and mainly Asian areas, suggesting that they are much more flexible in their preferences as to where they live. The city council is investigating this to find out more about this community's attitudes and housing aspirations.

- New migrant groups such as refugees or migrant workers might be entering the market in different ways and be making little use of social housing, even though they may be entitled to it. Their use of the private rented sector (for example) may change the market at local level or have an effect on house prices. For example, in South Lincolnshire, the survey of migrant workers and of the established population showed mainly positive local attitudes about migrants, but with concern about the impact on house prices as the private rented sector expands.

Monitoring change in local housing markets is therefore of critical importance to the development, implementation and review of a community cohesion strategy. Data collection needs to be based on three 'Ds':

- *Dynamic* – collected regularly and on an ongoing basis.
- *Diversity* – must be recognised: data must be available according to relevant ethnic divisions, household types, age, etc.
- *Disaggregated* – data must be available at neighbourhood level (as well as at higher levels).

3. How different neighbourhoods in the area work

Chapter 6 covered the issues about understanding individual neighbourhoods, in preparing for example for regeneration programmes. But it is also important to have a picture of neighbourhoods and how they work across an area (eg across a landlord's stock). Important questions include:

- What is the state of inter-community relations? This does not necessarily have to be measured by social surveys or other formal research methods, as envisaged for the official community cohesion indicators (see later in this chapter). Impressions can be obtained from frontline housing and community workers, local police officers, etc, who will often have built up a picture from their day-to-day dealings with people; via consultation with those representing particular communities, including refugee community organisations, and by routine monitoring of evidence on racist harassment.

- Whether those neighbourhoods that have become more mixed are also more cohesive; in other words, is there interaction between different groups and is it, on the whole, friendly?
- What is the level of contact between young and older people?
- How well do young people engage in local events and in attempts to consult the local communities?
- Where interaction between people of different ethnic groups does take place, does it involve just some ethnic groups or are all groups in contact?
- How far is the cohesiveness of neighbourhoods changing and how do different neighbourhoods compare? (The use of official indicators will be useful here.)
- Are some neighbourhoods resistant to change and to newcomers in their area?

4. Categorising neighbourhoods

The Commission has recommended that government bodies at central, regional and local level recognise that there are certain types of locality which present particular challenges in community cohesion and has proposed a 'typology' of at-risk areas across England (see Annex B of the Commission's report).

Housing organisations may want to create a typology at local level to help focus on key issues and areas. A possible typology for a large urban area outside London is shown below (see box). Different typologies will be needed in different areas. In smaller towns and cities, for example, there are often small areas of black and minority ethnic settlement near to the centre whereas other areas, apparently similar in housing terms, have far fewer people from minority communities. Changes in such areas need to be monitored. In addition to the ethnic composition, there may also be changes in the numbers and proportions of young people within the district as a whole and within particular areas that will need to be monitored.

In creating a typology, it is important to recognise that movement of households takes place across administrative boundaries. Local authorities should share information with each other and think about any requirement to commission research on a joint basis. Examples come from the work of the housing market renewal pathfinders. Bridging NewcastleGateshead has developed a community cohesion strategy built on a typology covering the whole pathfinder area and which divides it into different 'localities' such as those receiving new migrants, 'transforming' localities where tensions might occur and 'dormant' ones which are in decline.[105] This led into consideration of the different interventions appropriate to the different types of locality.

---

105 See *Promoting Equality and Sustainability through Housing Market Renewal* (downloadable at www.newcastlegatesheadpathfinder.co.uk).

Mapping changing neighbourhoods and communities –
a typology of areas for a large urban district

City or town centre housing
Housing in a number of city and town centres has been undergoing a renaissance over the last decade, but are the new apartments attracting a cross section of the local population? A Birmingham study of 'city living' carried out in 2007 found that 33.4% of residents in owner-occupied and private rented city centre properties (most of which are apartments built in the last 10 years) are from BME groups, with Indian, Chinese, Caribbean and 'Other White' being the main minority groups. This is a little higher than the proportion from BME communities in the city as a whole (approximately 30%).

Inner city mixed tenure housing
Often traditional areas of settlement for minority ethnic communities – but how far are they changing? Are white groups still moving out; or are they even moving back? How far are Indian households leaving, for example to be replaced by new communities arriving in the country? What evidence is there of community cohesion or community tensions?

Inner city council and housing association housing
Is the frequent over-representation of Black Caribbean households in these areas changing at all? Is the frequent under-representation of south Asian households changing? What is the pattern of demand for these areas?

Affluent suburbs of predominantly owner-occupied housing
How far is the ethnic composition of these areas changing? There is evidence that Indian households have been moving into these areas for some time, but are other minority groups now joining them? Are there areas where non-white people are effectively excluded?

Peripheral council estates
Traditionally, these areas have been predominantly white. Is this changing at all? What evidence is there of tensions about newcomers in these areas or of racist attitudes? If the areas are in decline, how does this impact on cohesion issues?

5. How cohesive neighbourhoods can be recognised
A strategy to bring about greater cohesion in a neighbourhood needs to develop some way of recognising what a cohesive neighbourhood looks like. What signs are there that one neighbourhood is more cohesive than another? How do we know whether the cohesiveness of a neighbourhood is increasing or not?

The call for 'strong and positive relationships' within neighbourhoods in *Community Cohesion: An action guide* seems to imply more than an absence of conflict. At their strongest and most positive, neighbourhood relationships involve mutual help – neighbours looking out for each other and providing practical support at times of difficulty – and active involvement in neighbourhood organisations. However, as we said in chapter 2, it is probably unrealistic to expect many neighbourhoods to develop these kinds of relationships and it is particularly unreasonable for policy makers to have this level of expectation, for example, for social housing estates or inner city areas when they would not have similar hopes for middle class suburbs or commuter villages.

The reality is that neighbourhoods will continue to exhibit a range of degrees of cohesiveness, with a spectrum running from a mere absence of conflict to deeply inclusive environments involving extensive participation and mutual help.

It would be useful to seek to identify reasons why some neighbourhoods are cohesive and some are not. A valuable piece of research would seek to compare neighbourhoods within a city or similar cities and identify what are the success factors and what are the issues that contribute to the difficulties and to consider how the lessons learned might be applied elsewhere.

6. Measuring cohesion at neighbourhood level

Cohesion is currently measured nationally by asking people the question:

> 'to what extent do you agree or disagree that this local area (within 15/20 minutes walking distance) is a place where people from different backgrounds get on well together?'

This is based on people's subjective sense of how relationships work in their local area. CLG Citizenship Surveys have found in both 2003 and 2005 that 80% of people in England and Wales perceived that people of different backgrounds got on well in their local areas.

The report *Building a Picture of Community Cohesion*[106] proposes an extra nine local indicators, with data being collected from both official statistics and from social surveys. Some relate directly to neighbourhoods or housing, and the ones most relevant to this guide are:

- The percentage of respondents who feel that they belong to their neighbourhood – part of a larger indicator that measures feeling part of the local area, the county and the country (CC02).
- Key priorities for improving an area – measured by asking respondents a question about the most important things that would make somewhere a good place to live and a further question about things that most need improving. 'Affordable decent housing' is one of the options given (CC03).

106 Home Office (2003).

- The percentage of people who feel that local ethnic differences are respected in their local area (CC05).
- The number of racial incidents recorded by police authorities per 100,000 people (CC06).
- The percentage of people from different backgrounds who mix with other people from different backgrounds in everyday situations. 'At a relative's home' and 'in your neighbourhood' are included in the options given (CC10).

Questions like these might be included in surveys for overall local cohesion strategies, but they might be selectively used as well as part of work in local neighbourhoods or to compare one neighbourhood with another. Further guidance is given in *Building a Picture of Community Cohesion*.

The Commission is recommending (para. 4.27) that there is a single national indicator of cohesion, but that local areas are also encouraged to develop their own indicators.

7. Finding out about attitudes to housing and neighbourhoods

Understanding the spatial dimension of preferences and constraints is of central importance. Widening housing opportunities for people depends crucially on knowing about their attitudes to different areas. The community cohesion agenda suggests a wider range of research questions than simply asking people where they wish to live.

The report *Breaking Down the Barriers* (see page 76) suggested a number of questions that might be asked about housing and neighbourhoods, including:

- Why people move out of, and to, particular areas.
- The way people think about different areas, why people choose the areas they do, whether people have heard of different areas and know anything about them, whether there are 'no go' areas, what defines a 'no go' area and what would change a 'no go' area into a 'go' area.
- How people balance living in a good home in an area they are not familiar with against having to wait longer for a home in an area they are familiar with.
- What influences people in their decisions about where they live and how sensitive the different factors are.
- How different options are perceived: knowledge of and views about different types of housing and housing providers, including shared ownership and co-operative housing.
- Preferences regarding living in mono-cultural or culturally-mixed communities (see box overleaf).
- What young people think about the housing that is available and the scale and appropriateness of facilities available to them.

Below are some findings from an earlier report on Bradford from one of the authors of *Breaking Down the Barriers*.

Views on living near own ethnic community – research findings from Bradford

Research on race and housing in Bradford identified a number of households of south Asian, African and Caribbean origin who wished to move home. These households were asked how important it was that they moved to an area where people of their own ethnic community lived.

Approximately seven out of ten south Asian households replied that it was either very or fairly important. In marked contrast, only 35% of African or Caribbean people felt it to be very or fairly important.

After acknowledging that the 30% of south Asians who regard ethnic composition as unimportant is perhaps higher than one might have assumed, the research goes on to demonstrate that south Asians favouring a local move were more likely to want to live in an area with people of their own ethnic community than those wishing to live away from their current area.

Source: Ratcliffe, P *et al* (1996) *'Race' and Housing in Bradford*. Bradford Housing Forum.

Answers to these kinds of questions could be sought through formal research projects, for example home interview surveys, but it also possible to tackle some of the issues in less formal ways. For example, housing associations engaged in 'expanding opportunities' schemes (see chapter 6) have to gauge the acceptability to people from ethnic minority communities of areas beyond 'traditional' settlement areas. This analysis may be carried out by a member of staff, with appropriate language skills, through home visits to a sample of people registered on waiting lists for housing.

8. The results of ethnic monitoring of service users
Ethnic monitoring has traditionally been used to measure the fairness of administrative systems. For example, the proportions of people from different ethnic groups applying for services (most frequently applications for tenancies) are compared with the proportions of those receiving services. Questions are then asked if there are disparities between the proportions. The debate about community cohesion raises a number of additional issues for ethnic monitoring:

- Do the data show that resources (eg available lettings) are allocated fairly between different communities?
- Are there changes in the areas where applicants from the various ethnic groups are requesting accommodation?

- Are bids from ethnic minority groups under choice-based lettings systems showing a different geographical pattern of preferences compared with that established by traditional waiting lists?
- Is the pattern of lettings to BME groups changing in geographical terms? The need to combine data on local authority and housing association lettings should be considered.

Housing-specific data – such as CORE returns, data in support of performance indicators, etc – are useful sources but organisations should check that they cover the important issues from a 'cohesion' perspective and also that they reflect the current local demographic situation. As far as possible, attempts should also be made to collect information about the ethnicity and age of alleged perpetrators of harassment and anti-social behaviour and of the parties involved in neighbourhood disputes.

Main elements of a community cohesion and housing strategy

On the basis of the kinds of information and analysis mentioned in the previous section on 'Understanding the Local Context', housing organisations should be able to develop their own strategic approach to community cohesion, whether (as discussed earlier) this is a separate strategy or is part of a wider approach.

The previous chapters in the guide have set out the key elements:

- creating strong and positive relationships within neighbourhoods
- creating more mixed neighbourhoods
- investing for cohesive neighbourhoods.

The emphasis to be placed on each of these will vary between housing organisations. Changes within the organisation itself, and in its relationship with other bodies, may also be needed as part of the strategy. This issue will be covered in chapter 8.

Partners and, wherever possible, community representatives should be involved in the task of identifying and appraising options for promoting better community cohesion through the strategy. There are alternatives both for what is done and who should do it.

Here are some of the other ways in which the community cohesion strategy might interface with mainstream housing work:

- *Use of resources*. A view needs to be taken of resource distribution (eg lettings, sites for and types of new build) in relation to the needs of different communities. Can the organisation demonstrate that it is acting fairly (eg that lettings roughly match the make-up of the local population) and that one community is not getting a disproportionate share?
- *Priorities for investment*. In new development or regeneration, priorities need to be considered from a community cohesion perspective, and this discussed with

funding and partner agencies. If major investment is taking place, a specific cohesion strategy may be needed to guide policies and implementation. (Good examples have been produced by some of the housing market renewal pathfinders.)[107]

- *Choice of partners*. Options regarding the different agencies to be involved in delivering programmes also need to be evaluated. There are clear advantages arising from the involvement of BME-led housing associations in the creation of new settlement areas. But the role of other providers should also be evaluated, including mainstream housing associations and private developers, and the experience in community cohesion which they might offer.

- *Stock transfer proposals*. Consideration might be given to transfers of stock to BME-led housing associations or to mainstream associations who will work in partnership with BME HAs (see example on page 142).

- *Stock rationalisation proposals*. In making decisions about rationalisation of ownership or management in multi-landlord areas, the impact on cohesion needs to be considered.

- *Community empowerment*. If proposals are being developed in line with the local government white paper (see chapter 5), is there scope for initiatives to encourage local communities, including BME communities, to take more control of their housing or of their neighbourhoods?

One approach to ensuring that cohesion becomes a criterion in all aspects of an organisation's work is to 'cohesion proof' all policies and proposals. An example of doing this is provided by the Gloucestershire LSP.

Gloucester Partnership's Community Cohesion Proofing Tool

Gloucester Partnership developed the proofing tool to try to:

- minimise mistakes made through generalisation, by bringing national, regional and local knowledge into one useful focus

- promote interdepartmental, interagency and partnership working, and the sharing of information and good practice where appropriate

- promote inclusion, not exclusion.

The proofing tool is a list of questions to be asked about policies or proposals, aimed at testing their impact on cohesion and whether this has been considered in designing them. It is available to (but not imposed on) the partner agencies in the LSP.

More information: www.gloucesterpartnership.org.uk

---

107 For example, the strategy for the Bridging NewcastleGateshead pathfinder *Promoting Equality and Sustainability through Housing Market Renewal* (downloadable at www.newcastlegatesheadpathfinder.co.uk).

Implementing the strategy

An action plan, written with specific, measurable, agreed and time-bound (SMART) objectives, is an essential part of any strategy. Plans need to communicate absolute clarity about what is to be done, by whom and when.

Commitment to the strategy can be secured by:

- managers putting initial effort into explaining to staff and to those involved from partner organisations why the strategy has been devised and what contribution to implementation is expected from each team/organisation
- ensuring that the strategy forms part of training programmes
- designating a cabinet or board member as a community cohesion 'champion'
- requiring that reports to cabinets, boards and committees contain an assessment of any community cohesion implications.

Implementation will invariably need to be phased with learning from experience built in to inform later phases. The need for formal experiments and pilot projects should be considered. 'Quick win' initiatives help to build credibility for the strategy.

Deploying resources

Achieving change on the scale necessary to bring about truly cohesive neighbourhoods must inevitably involve a review of how resources are used. New activities need to be funded in some way and there may be changes to the priority accorded to different kinds of housing development initiatives.

The following are some of the resource implications of community cohesion and housing strategies:

- Housing developments that add to the ethnic diversity of particular areas may need to be prioritised.
- Consideration will need to be given to the principle that projects will not be funded unless they can demonstrate that they comply with community cohesion objectives – this may have a cost.
- New funding programmes, or changes in the focus of existing funding programmes, may be needed to support social landlords' efforts to promote contact between people of different ethnic groups and to implement initiatives that involve and empower young people.
- Resource allocation mechanisms must be transparent and the results monitored and published in order to avoid inter-community friction.

It must be born in mind that, despite its importance, there is no specific funding stream for implementing a cohesion strategy – only what can be devoted to it from mainstream programmes. It is therefore essential that the organisation's leaders – boards, cabinet members, directors or chief executives – recognise not only that the task is important but that resources must be found to carry it out (see chapter 8).

Publishing the strategy

The essential aim of any strategy is the achievement of real change, not the production of a document. However, a published version is needed to assist communication. The aim is not to produce a lengthy document just for the sake of it. Documents need to be fit for the purpose. There are different ways in which a strategy for housing and community cohesion can be set out – as a stand-alone document or as a section on community cohesion in other strategy documents, perhaps with a separate community cohesion and housing action plan.

Whatever is decided about the method of publication, at the least an outline of the local approach to cohesion should be included in the housing strategy document.

Monitoring and evaluation

Early thought should be given as to how the strategy will be monitored and evaluated since this helps to focus minds on recognisable outcomes. The key question is: how will we know whether the strategy is working?

The community cohesion indicators mentioned earlier will need to be monitored. So will targets set out in the action plan. Accountability can be built in if people responsible for implementing elements of the plan are required to report regularly to a forum on which community and partner representatives are present. The need for a comprehensive evaluation, perhaps carried out by an independent person or organisation, should be considered.

However, getting a real picture of how cohesive different neighbourhoods are, and how they are changing, is not an easy task. A practitioner consulted in preparing this guide commented:

> *'The idea that targets can be developed and results measured can be very simplistic. In practice it is incredibly difficult. People choose where to live. We can encourage mixed and cohesive neighbourhoods and try to provide the right conditions, but we can't force it. For example, ethnic clustering has grown organically around available facilities. The factors which influence choice are often outside our control, eg churches, mosques, etc.'*

This is a reminder that any strategy has to be firmly grounded in the reality of day-to-day circumstances in estates and neighbourhoods where it is being applied.

Community cohesion and housing strategies: organisational responsibilities for a local authority strategy

Local authority – overall strategy

- carries out baseline assessment of how current policies and programmes promote community cohesion
- develops community cohesion strategy setting out a vision for the area and an action plan for achieving it

Local Strategic Partnership

- prepares (or helps local authority with the preparation and implementation of) the Sustainable Community Strategy
- pulls together local strategies to look at how they are complementing each other in building cohesive communities

Regional housing board

- decides on broad geographical and thematic priorities for investment, including identifying broad areas where investment could bring about more racially-mixed communities

Local authority housing department

- takes lead in developing a community cohesion and housing
- puts community cohesion and housing issues on to relevant agendas
- influences priorities set by regional housing board
- sets more precise geographical and thematic priorities for investment
- implements the strategy

Local authority planning department

- develops policies to influence the tenure, size, type and affordability of housing
- produces Local Development Framework and associated plans

Housing partners – housing associations, private developers, etc.

- help to develop the strategy
- share in implementing the strategy.

Checklist on community cohesion strategies

✓ Are local authorities taking the lead in work on community cohesion? If not, are housing associations discussing the best way of getting the issues onto the agenda locally?

✓ Has a strategy for community cohesion and housing been drawn up in consultation with communities and partners?

✓ Have housing data been included in the local authority community cohesion baseline assessment that needs to be carried out?

✓ Have housing staff been involved in work on collecting the data for the community cohesion indicators?

✓ Has a review been carried out of research and intelligence gathering to ensure that relevant information on housing and community cohesion is being collected?

✓ Has an action plan on community cohesion and housing been produced that clearly sets out who is to do what and when?

✓ Are arrangements in place to monitor and evaluate the community cohesion and housing strategy?

CHAPTER 8

ROLES, RESPONSIBILITIES AND PARTNERSHIPS

What this chapter is about:

- responsibilities for community cohesion
- promoting community cohesion within housing organisations
- wider work to promote community cohesion
- working with communities

The responsibility to achieve more cohesive communities

As we indicated in chapter 2, all housing organisations have legal obligations to avoid discriminatory and segregationist practices. They need to ensure that the services they offer are appropriate to the needs and preferences of the range of ethnic groups that exist in, or who may be seeking to move to, their areas of operation. They should ensure that their practices maximise opportunities and choice for an increasingly diverse population. These are the starting points for any serious attempt to create cohesive neighbourhoods.

But the Commission also calls on public services to 'mainstream' integration and cohesion into their activities, with locally-determined measures to be judged (for example) as part of the new Comprehensive Area Assessments for local authorities. Increasingly, therefore, housing organisations will be judged by the extent to which they champion, not just equality of treatment, but also more cohesive communities.

This chapter is about the task of 'mainstreaming' cohesion, and what that means for housing bodies. It looks first at the responsibilities which different bodies have, then at their work within – and outside – their organisations. Finally it looks at their work with communities.

Responsibilities of housing organisations

The strategic housing role

The community cohesion agenda presents a set of challenges for the strategic housing and enabling activities of local authorities. Staff engaged in these areas may well lead the work on community cohesion and housing strategies. They need to be familiar with the policy developments taking place nationally and the guidance given here. They have a key role in linking work on community cohesion in housing with the wider corporate work on the issue. They need to ensure that issues set out in the Sustainable Community Strategy and the work of Local Strategic Partnerships are translated into housing objectives.

They also have responsibilities for getting community cohesion issues onto the agenda of consultative forums with partners and residents, for ensuring that appropriate research is carried out and for building analysis and proposals into appropriate strategy documents, including the local housing strategy. They should seek to broker new ways of partnership working to deliver community cohesion objectives. They should scrutinise policy initiatives and proposals for new programmes to ensure that they do not run counter to community cohesion principles.

A further task relates to the need for initiatives to widen opportunities for people from BME communities to live away from traditional settlement areas. Staff in strategy and enabling teams should discuss proposals with potential providers, including housing associations. Active consideration should be given to the role that should be played by BME-led housing associations in the provision or management of housing beyond traditional settlement areas. It would be the role of strategy and enabling officers to review options for the transfer of existing social housing to BME-led associations in potential new settlement areas – to increase the numbers of houses that might be attractive to communities looking for wider housing opportunities.

In partnership with colleagues from other departments, such as regeneration, economic development and planning, they should consider the role that regeneration initiatives could play in changing the balance of the stock in particular areas in a way that may attract a wider range of ethnic groups.

They should ensure they are consulted by planning officers about policies to facilitate an appropriate mix of homes in terms of type, size and affordability in new developments. They should also make sure that consideration is given by planners in design guides on residential development to the need for new housing to be based on principles that reduce friction between neighbours, facilitate sociability and make neighbourhoods secure (see chapter 6).

They also need to enter into dialogue with the full range of social and private sector housing organisations working in their district to ensure that good practice is adopted. They should challenge practices that are discriminatory and segregationist.

Social landlords

The guide has focused on three key areas of the landlord role – promoting better relationships at neighbourhood level, achieving more mixed neighbourhoods and achieving greater cohesion through new investment opportunities. It has also tried to show how landlords need to build integration and cohesion into their day-to-day tasks of managing and repairing their housing stock. Some further aspects will be dealt with in this chapter.

Whether or not a landlord has a strategic responsibility for community cohesion of the kind discussed in chapter 7, all landlords should test the extent to which their activities contribute to cohesion and have policies for promoting it – possibly as an integral part of their race equality schemes. They also need to ensure that cohesion is imbued in the work of the organisation, from board or cabinet level down to frontline staff and work with residents. This chapter covers the remaining areas that landlords need to consider.

Black and minority ethnic housing associations

BME-led housing associations can play a particular role in delivering the community cohesion agenda. Their potential role is not only the provision and management of accommodation but also the wider issues of building and supporting communities and of promoting inter-community contact and trust, discussed earlier in the guide. They also have a role as 'diversity champions' within localities, raising issues and helping other organisations (including other associations) to develop services that are appropriate to diverse communities.

Although most BME associations will want to maintain links with the communities that they originally identified closely with, the community cohesion agenda has raised the question for all of them about diversification of their areas of operation. The creation of new opportunities for minority communities in the future will mean, in most cases, the development and acquisition of housing away from traditional areas, with the result that, as time goes by, the associations' stock will become more geographically dispersed.

Many BME associations have widened their areas of operation and some are actively involved in community cohesion programmes – there are examples in the CIH/Housing Corporation study *The Future of BME Housing Associations*.[108] But the pace of change

---

108 Lupton, M and Perry, J (2004). CIH.

has increased. The involvement of BME associations in the remodelling of local authority estates, their acquisition of stock through transfer – either of local authority housing or from other associations through trickle transfer, rationalisation or other arrangements – has meant diversification of the associations' areas of operation, together with a widening customer base. An example is the creation of Firebird JVC Ltd in Bradford, and the partnership between Manningham, a BME-led HA, and other HA partners in the city (see box).

BME associations have had to review whether their image, board and staff profiles and range of services are still appropriate to the wider range of communities that they increasingly serve – for example, people from Black Caribbean and African backgrounds and those from refugee and migrant communities. Many such as Manningham are actively working with refugee communities – and there are further examples in the CIH guide *Housing and Support Services for Asylum Seekers and Refugees*. Of the six partnerships involved in the hact/CIH *Opening Doors* project, two are BME-led and are working with refugee or new migrant communities.

Bradford Partnership aims to create mixed communities in new build schemes

Bradford Community Housing Trust (BCHT) has entered into a formal agreement with four local housing associations: Accent Group, Leeds Federated, Manningham Housing Association (MHA) and Unity Housing, to create Firebird JVC Ltd, a joint-venture company to undertake new build and regeneration work. Firebird will build new homes for BCHT on sites created on land on their estates. Many of these developments are to be managed in partnership with MHA, which has experience of encouraging people from diverse communities to apply for housing in unfamiliar areas, and in delivering culturally-sensitive services.

The aim is to meet the increasing demand for affordable housing and encourage mixed communities in the district. The outcomes anticipated include:

* balanced, mixed communities, sustainable in the long term
* attracting new tenants from more diverse communities
* meeting BME needs in non-traditional BME locations
* removal of barriers to BME access to social housing
* culturally-sensitive services for the new tenants
* greater community involvement and tenant participation.

Construction work has started on a number of sites and the properties will be let through Bradford's CBL scheme, Homehunter (see page 84).

Further information: Jake Piergies, Strategic Partnerships Officer, 01274 254295.

In view of their track record of culturally-sensitive provision and the level of trust from minority communities, there should be a clear role for BME-led associations working with other associations, including as part of group structures. There are several examples of this, one being the way that Ashram HA, which is part of the Accord Group, has influenced the work of other group members in working with minority ethnic communities.[109] Many BME associations are already engaged in similar work, as is clear from several of the examples in this guide.

Private housing bodies

There have already been examples in the guide of the way that the private sector can contribute to the cohesion agenda. It is unlikely that private bodies will adopt explicit objectives about community cohesion but they may well have 'signed up' to a wider agenda of social mix and achieving sustainable communities, if they are engaged in regeneration or new build schemes in partnership with social landlords or (for example) through section 106 agreements, or if they are bidding for the National Affordable Housing Programme and have to meet its requirements (see page 28).

One developer consulted in preparing this guide pointed to efforts to market a development to different Asian communities, and to the Irish community, in different parts of London where this made sense commercially. They were nervous of explicitly committing to achieving ethnic mix in their projects but at the same time welcomed a socially-diverse mix of residents, believing that in the long term it made the developments more sustainable.

Many developers and firms in the building industry are willing to support the advantages of a diverse workforce. There is guidance in the Summit Skills *Diversity Handbook* for the building industry, with examples and quotes from firms committed to diversity.[110] Developers working with social sector landlords can be expected to have equality or diversity policies, and show that they take their (more limited) legal obligations seriously, are following good practice, and have ways of showing that their practices work.

Promoting community cohesion within organisations

Governance

Good governance is the lynchpin of an efficient and effective housing organisation. Boards of housing associations or cabinet members and portfolio holders in local

---

109 Details are given in *The Future of BME Housing Associations*, p.54.
110 Available from the Summit Skills website
     (www.summitskills.org.uk/public/downloads/DiversityHandbook.pdf).

authorities should strive to show leadership and forward thinking and planning for their business. Ownership of integration and cohesion policies by boards, cabinet members and chief executives or directors of housing organisations is essential if they are to promote them effectively in every aspect of their business and through all their staff.

This means much more than simply having a paragraph assessing the 'equality implications' of a housing programme or policy change. Atul Patel, chief executive of LHA-ASRA, has said that:[111]

> *'Diversity is about much more than strategies, awareness training, action plans and tick boxes. To be effective, the commitment set by boards and executives must be heartfelt: it's about vision, culture and tone.'*

It means finding a multiplicity of ways to imbue integration and cohesion in the organisation's work. For example:

- Creating a board or (in the case of local authorities) seeking councillors who represent the diverse communities in the area served by the organisation.
- Having a housing and community cohesion strategy (chapter 7) which is 'owned' by the board/cabinet, has output targets which are reviewed, and which is championed on public occasions, not hidden away.
- Getting cross-party agreement wherever possible (for example, in Sheffield there is cross-party agreement to the city's refugee strategy).
- Ensuring that (as the Commission points out) creating cohesive communities is seen as an across-the-board issue, not one which only concerns ethnic minorities or is relevant only in certain parts of an area.
- Trying to be 'ahead of the game' – developing intelligence about change in communities and tensions that might emerge or are beginning to do so. Thinking 'outside the box' to devise ways to defuse tensions or at least anticipate them (see the Waltham Forest example on page 50).
- Looking for the community cohesion potential in apparently unrelated areas of work – for example developing neighbourhood warden schemes (see pages 55 and 58) or devising a new lettings policy (page 78).
- Wanting to understand the customer base – and potential customer base – within the area, and how to engage effectively with all customers.

Two examples of corporate commitment come from very different areas – Tower Hamlets in London and St Vincent's HA in the North West.

---

111 *Inside Housing*, 18 May 2007.

Commitment to equality and cohesion in Tower Hamlets

The London Borough of Tower Hamlets has one of the most racially-diverse communities in the country, with 49% coming from minority ethnic backgrounds, 66% of whom are Bangladeshi. Both the council and the LSP see equality and cohesion as central to the quality of life for everyone in the borough.

A corporate policy of 'quality services for everyone' aims to reduce the risk of perceived unfair allocation of resources, and of intercommunity resentment. Given the level of diversity in the borough and the number of people who do not speak English as a first language, the council established bilingual posts in key services to better meet local language needs and reduce translation costs. Having bilingual staff also gives a positive message about the council being an equal opportunities employer that values fluency in a minority language as a communication skill, while building a workforce that is reflective of the wider community. About 30% of the staff in the council's Customer Contact Centre are bilingual.

The council's weekly newspaper *Eastend Life* is the most widely-read local newspaper among the borough's minority ethnic communities and includes pages written in English with a summary of key points in community languages. Pictorial messages are used for those who lack English language skills or who have basic literacy needs.

Source: *Integration and Cohesion Case Studies*, p.218.

Corporate commitment in St Vincent's HA

St Vincent's is a medium-sized HA operating in the North West, mainly in ethnically-diverse areas. It is a participant in the hact/CIH *Opening Doors* project and is committed to improving its services to refugees and new migrant groups.

There is strong commitment from the board and chief executive. This is matched by strong personal commitment from key managers. A board champion has been appointed with terms of reference for the role of expanding services to refugees/new migrants. Equality and diversity training is compulsory for all staff and encouraged for all board members. A proposal to expand this training to include awareness training on asylum seekers, refugees and new migrants is being actively considered.

All jobs are advertised in the ethnic minority press and on the COFEM website.[112] Secondments are encouraged and there is a commitment to PATH trainees (currently three) to ensure that people from different communities obtain the skills to compete at all levels within the employment market.

The ethnic background of contractors is assessed and reported to the board. Working as part of the Northern Lights Consortium, a local labour agreement is under review, aiming to increase the number of BME contractors.

Further information: www.svha.org.uk

---

112 'Career Opportunities for Ethnic Minorities' (see www.housingdiversitynetwork.co.uk/mentoring/default.asp).

Making the business case

Boards and cabinets are more likely to endorse cohesion strategies and allocate resources if they see the business case for doing so. It may seem obvious that seeking to promote services to all potential customers, or working to create positive relationships within an estate, are in the long-term business interests of the organisation, but this needs spelling out. For example, the Audit Commission's evaluation of housing market renewal pathfinders criticised them for their 'limited response' to the issue.[113] An example was a pathfinder that stressed the key importance of BME households to the local market but which had only recently studied their housing aspirations. The Commission said that this pathfinder was 'failing its BME communities'.

The advantages of making a serious commitment to community cohesion are not necessarily obvious, while the risks may be. The case needs to be made, stressing the potential costs of *not* having a commitment to cohesion as well as the likely gains.

Workforce

As can be seen from the examples above, commitment to a workforce which reflects the community in which the organisation is based is important both for practical reasons (like availability of language skills) and for reasons of the image which is presented to customers and potential customers. The Commission calls (in para. 4.33) for organisations to have action plans for targeted recruitment, and to improve opportunities for women workers.

Part of the reason for the success of Bradford's Homehunter lettings scheme (see page 84) is thought to be the positive efforts which were made to recruit more ethnically-diverse staff to deal with customers. Bradford Community Housing Trust has also recruited women into its repairs service so that female tenants can request a women-only team if (for example) they live alone.

Bradford Building Services (BBS)

BBS is Bradford Community Housing Trust's repair and maintenance service, handling 50,000 repairs per year. BBS actively recruits apprentices from across the district's communities including the inner city areas. The organisation works closely with schools and colleges to promote construction apprenticeships. BBS aims to achieve a diverse workforce, break down stereotypes about building workers and encourage applicants from under-represented communities to join the service.

→

---

113 Audit Commission (2006) *Housing Market Renewal: Annual Review 2005/06*, paras. 183-191.

Three years ago BBS had difficulty in attracting applicants from under-represented groups of the community to fill vacancies. Recently there have been over 300 applicants for seven apprenticeships, a reflection of the new approaches to recruitment.

Further information: www.bchtgroup.org/equal-opportunities.html

Training

Although most social landlords have programmes of training in equalities and diversity issues, these do not necessarily include the importance of community cohesion in the organisation's work and the contribution which all staff (and board members/councillors) should make. For example, are staff aware of the cohesion agenda and their expected role in it? Are those with management or strategic responsibilities familiar with the key documents mentioned in this guide? Is there discussion about what cohesion means in specific contexts, and are there opportunities to generate ideas about how to promote it?

Training programmes may also fail to keep up with the organisation's changing customer base. For example, an evaluation of a community cohesion pathfinder scheme in Brent in 2004 said that staff had a profound lack of knowledge about the communities that make up West London:[114]

> *'Although the influx of Somalis started more than ten years ago the officers present at the workshop had little knowledge of their culture or background.'*

This lack of knowledge was said to have extended from the community level into the heart of statutory authorities which are committed to serving all communities equally. This was an important handicap, not least because familiarity with existing communities, matched by early recognition of the development of new communities, helps to meet new service demands in a managed way and to avoid tension growing between new and existing communities.

It is vital that the intelligence which organisations gather so as to better understand and serve changing communities (see chapter 7) feeds through into staff briefings and other formal and informal communication channels. The CIH guide *Housing and Support Services for Asylum Seekers and Refugees* points to the example of a comment by a frontline housing worker that 'we don't have enough houses to allocate because there are so many asylum seekers', which should be as unacceptable as a similar comment made about black people.

---

114 Leask, P (2004) *Bringing Communities Closer: A report on the work of the West London Community Cohesion Pathfinder.*

Notting Hill's 'Love where you work' forum

At Notting Hill Housing Trust an internal cultural and faith awareness-raising programme has been delivered by a cross-section of staff through a variety of projects and campaigns. The programme aims to raise individual awareness and also impact on the frontline services provided to customers. As staff also belong to their own communities, such awareness and respect should filter back to local level. Examples of action taken include a calendar for all staff highlighting different religions for each month of the year, and a poster campaign focusing on the religious and cultural beliefs of each of the main communities housed by the trust. The trust also makes the reality of its diverse workforce clear on its website and in its recruitment process.

Further information: JHilditch@nhhg.org.uk

Procurement and commissioning

Most housing organisations will have equality and diversity policies that apply to their own working and to issues such as procurement. It is worth ensuring that these include community cohesion considerations. For example, do contractors and suppliers have policies to ensure that they have a diverse workforce that reflects the communities with which they work? Are tendering lists framed in such a way that BME contractors can gain access to them? If services are being commissioned (eg under Supporting People), are small, community-based organisations being considered because of their capacity to engage with particular groups which otherwise might not make use of the services? If such bodies lack the capacity to engage in this way, are there ways of helping them develop their capacity or linking them with bigger organisations?[115] Three examples of community cohesion principles being followed in procurement are:

- Metropolitan Housing Partnership have diversity training programmes for their repairs and maintenance contractors, influenced by residents' views on what they expect of contractors (see www.mhp-online.co.uk/diversity.html).

- Southern Housing Group has also set up training programmes for contractors, covering (for instance) gender issues and how to enter tenants' homes (see www.southernhousinggroup.co.uk/ourkeypolicies.asp?policy=10).[116]

- The London Borough of Haringey (see example on page 158) positively develops the capacity of small providers in its Supporting People programme.

---

115 On commissioning community-based organisations, see the guide by hact (forthcoming, 2008) *More Responsive Public Services? – A guide to commissioning migrant and refugee community organisations.* JRF.

116 On these and similar initiatives in repairs services, there will be an online resource published by HouseMark (www.housemark.co.uk) in 2008 provisionally entitled *Embracing Diversity in Repairs and Maintenance.*

The Singh Commission raised specific concerns about funding of community-based organisations ('single group funding') and this issue is dealt with in appendix 1.

Wider work to promote community cohesion

Partnerships

It is routine to emphasise the importance of partnership working, but in community cohesion it really is vital, as the examples in the guide have demonstrated. Housing organisations are not expected, and in many cases cannot, work alone. Some of the issues about successful partnership working are these:

- *Get 'buy in' to community cohesion* at a high enough level in each partner to secure adequate commitment of time and resources to it.
- *Involve all key partners in creating a strategy at the outset* rather than expecting them to agree to one already developed.
- *Try to 'map' all those bodies which have an interest in this area of work* and may want to be partners. Many agencies will already be working on issues to do with community cohesion, even if they don't give it that label.
- *Ensure there is adequate staff time and resources* outside day-to-day workloads.
- *Suggest staff exchanges* which might improve understanding between partners.
- *Be open-minded about the possibility of working across boundaries* depending on the local circumstances and issues.
- *Consider how the strategy will be 'kept on track'* so that it really meets the targets expressed, and makes effective use of resources.
- *Consider how communities themselves can best be involved*, and whether any potential partners have already begun such work (eg with new migrant communities).

It is worth mentioning that housing does not have an automatic 'place at the table' as far as community cohesion is concerned. For example, the 14 community cohesion pathfinders which took place in the follow up to the Cantle report rarely had housing elements.[117] Housing organisations may have to seek partners who are already working in this area – and this is where housing associations may have a particular role, especially (for example) in an authority which has transferred its stock.

Most of the examples in the guide have been partnerships to deliver services, projects or schemes. There have also been examples of strategic partnerships such as Southampton's new migrants strategy (page 121) where housing organisations have had a key role. Here are two further examples, again from contrasting environments.

---

117 See Robinson, D (2004) *How Housing Management can Contribute to Community Cohesion*. CIH.

West London Community Cohesion Partnership

Hounslow Council coordinates the sub-regional West London Community Cohesion Partnership, consisting of six local authorities of Hounslow, Ealing, Harrow, Hillingdon, Hammersmith and Fulham, and Brent; and has been instrumental in shaping multi-agency work on cohesion across West London. Partners include: West London Housing, the police, health agencies and media groups (Trinity Mirror Group), the voluntary sector (West London Network) and the private sector (West London Business).

The partnership recognised that a strong sub-regional approach was needed to tackle some of the barriers to cohesion and integration relating to communications, contingency planning, social exclusion, mainstreaming and extremism. The council is developing a sophisticated delivery model – at local and sub-regional levels on these issues and others, as outlined in the Hounslow Community Plan 2007-2010. The model highlights ways of working that mainstream cohesion in the council's work. Hounslow's Community Cohesion Strategy Group is currently developing performance indicators, which include actual and perceived levels of tension.

The council is leading on a study on far right ideology and religious fundamentalism. It robustly addressed myths perpetuated by far right groups that actively target the area, and make efforts to connect with disengaged, deprived white groups. Hounslow Council is currently managing a £600,000 sub-regional pathfinder programme to prevent violent extremism.

Further information: sabin.malik@hounslow.gov.uk

Cornwall Strategic Partnership Migrant Workers Group

This partnership has been recognised as one of the best examples of a multi-agency approach towards dealing with the issues around recent EU migration. Along with its comprehensive 'Welcome to Cornwall' pack and responsible employers scheme, the partnership is leading on a shared database of local accommodation providers, and developing a responsible landlord scheme.

The welcome pack has proved to be very effective, and it has been distributed throughout Cornwall, to neighbouring counties, and even to would-be migrant workers through recruitment agencies. Employers use it widely.

The Migrant Workers Group has been the driver behind the inclusion of migrant worker issues in the LAA.

→

The multi-agency West Cornwall Migrant Workers Action Group (MIGWAG) has a shared information database which holds details of employers, providers of accommodation, numbers of workers, nationalities, gangmaster activities, and conditions found upon inspection. This protocol allows partners to identify, prevent and manage incidents of crime and ASB committed against or by migrant workers. It is also used for inspection of sites providing accommodation in the form of caravans. The aim is to so ensure a satisfactory standard of accommodation and the health, safety and welfare of the workers.

Source: *Integration and Cohesion Case Studies*, p129.

Communications

An effective communications strategy is fundamental to community cohesion, and the Commission puts particular emphasis on communication with long-established communities and finding out how they get their information about crucial issues such as levels of immigration and how scarce resources are allocated. The strategy needs to be directed as much at frontline workers and people such as councillors as it does to the media or the public at large.

The key requirements identified by the Commission are:

- *Knowledge* – an organisation which is well-informed about the communities it serves is less likely to be caught out by criticisms based on misconception or half truths (eg 'this tower block is full of refugees').

- *Transparency* – the organisation's commitment to fairness in use of resources (eg letting houses) must be accompanied by openness and the ready availability of facts.

- *Positive messages* – for example, about the value of migrant workers in the local economy or the performance of schools which have accepted asylum seeker children.

- *Rapid rebuttal* – of false stories. It is vital that organisations can respond rapidly and with authority to false accusations or rumours that are easy to make and less easily damped down. There need to be arrangements for commenting outside office hours, and avoiding responses such as 'we do not comment on individual applications'.

Taking this further, a communication strategy for handling a sensitive topic such as community cohesion should have the following elements:

- *Adequate planning for and resourcing of communications* – there needs to be a commitment throughout the organisation and communication must be seen as a core task, as important to frontline staff as to senior managers.

- *Clear and shared responsibilities* – as mentioned earlier, board members and elected members need to be signed up to policies on community cohesion, and need to be briefed in key issues in case they are called to make comments by the press or within communities. In partnerships, lines of external communication need to be part of any working agreement.

- *Recognising the value of positive media relations* – the media can be an ally in changing minds about (for example) the value of new migration or the reputation of a poor neighbourhood. Local media, in particular, have a stake in the area and an interest in positive images. (In this respect they are often different from the national press).

- *Having a preventative approach to potential problems* – as the Commission says (para. 7.27), allocation of resources is a sensitive issue. Having a strategy which recognises this throughout will help to make it less sensitive. We have already discussed (page 133) ways in which resources can be distributed so that different communities feel they are getting a fair share. This needs to be reflected too in the way actions are presented to the press and to the public at large.

- *Establishing trust with local communities* – the most damaging stories occur when the press is able to portray communities as being ignored or having valid views which are not being acted upon. Effort needs to be made to build trust, so that community representatives have more to gain from talking directly to the organisation rather than using the press (see Peterborough example below).

- *Building positive relations with local media* – the Commission makes several comments about working with the media, recommending (para. 7.22) that local bodies try positively to engage local media in the structures they establish to promote community cohesion. There are successful examples of this in Birmingham and Leicester, which have led to changed presentation of ethnic minorities in the press, and to reduced opportunities for racist views to be expressed.

An example of a positive strategy with clear political leadership comes from Peterborough (see box). A resource for work with communities, young people, etc on migration issues, called 'Where Our Journeys Meet', has been produced by the West Midlands Strategic Migration Partnership (see www.wmlga.gov.uk/page.asp?id=510).

The Singh Commission raised specific concerns about translations and this issue is dealt with in appendix 2.

A positive communications strategy – Peterborough City Council

Multi-agency work to manage migration in Peterborough initially resulted in a barrage of negative media stories, with headlines such as 'Call for action over influx of refugees' and 'Racial fears over placing of asylum centre'.

In response, councillors took the lead in promoting positive messages about the city's need to fill skill shortages and ability to cope with new migrants. Local residents and migrants and refugees were identified to tell their personal experiences. Media training was given to community group leaders so they could develop direct relationships with the media and promote positive stories. The council's own media team were given awareness training so that they were better placed to stop misinformation circulating about migrants and refugees. Other agencies, such as the police, were involved. The council also used a range of channels to promote the benefits to the local economy of new communities moving in.

This activity had real impact. Headlines became more positive, for example, 'The Culture Shock – and why there is more to unite us than there is to divide us' and 'City has too few jobless to fill posts' were stories that painted a better picture.

More information from the New Link Asylum and Migration Service at Peterborough City Council – www.peterborough.gov.uk/page-3838

Myth busting

'Myth busting' is especially important – in working with the media, with communities and with the organisation's own staff – and therefore warrants separate coverage. The Commission is clear on the importance of fairness in responding to community tensions:

> *'When the majority believe there is a problem, there are three broad options in response – pander to their fears by taking draconian action towards the newcomers, work with them to address the legitimate concerns that they have, or try to show them that their fears are unfounded. Our fear is that in the current climate, the majority will be pandered to, with immigrant rights being removed or freedoms being restricted. We therefore want to see work that either defuses the issue or dispels the myth – and the key to this is communication.'* (para. 7.25)

The Commission calls for myth busting strategies aimed at established local communities, with accurate and impartial facts about recent population changes and the benefits of migration. It suggests 'face-to-face dialogue' with communities most likely to believe myths.

The box overleaf gives sources of guidance or examples of approaches to media contacts and myth busting.

Sources of guidance on the media and 'myth busting'

'Reporting Diversity'

The Society of Editors has produced a downloadable guide to diversity issues and how the media can contribute to community cohesion.

Downloadable at: www.societyofeditors.co.uk/pageview.php?page_id=191&parent_page_id=141

'Communicating Community Cohesion'

The IDeA website has a toolkit with numerous examples of working with the media and myth busting:

See: www.idea.gov.uk/idk/core/page.do?pageId=5782974#intro

The press and refugees

The Refugee Council publishes advice on tackling press distortions about asylum seekers and refugees, and also has guidelines which the press should be following.

See: www.refugeecouncil.org.uk

Defeating organised racial hatred

The Commission for Racial Equality has a downloadable set of resource packs giving both general guidance, and specific information relating to issues such as Islamophobia and hatred towards Gypsies and Travellers.

Further information: www.cre.gov.uk/about/sci_index.html

MediaWise Trust

The MediaWise Trust argues for responsible press reporting, and has advice on treatment of refugees in the media. Its archive has a wide range of material on different aspects of prejudice or misrepresentation, for example of disabled people, Gypsies and Travellers, etc.

Further information: www.presswise.org.uk

Dealing with the media

The Refugee Media Group in Wales has produced a downloadable guide, especially aimed at refugee community organisations. It has 'grassroots' experience from Wales, and advice for refugees on being interviewed and getting their stories across to the media.

Downloadable via: www.icar.webbler.co.uk/?lid=4745

Having the media as partners

In the West London Community Cohesion Pathfinder, the Trinity Mirror media group were partners and helped both to train local people in media techniques and worked with local newspapers to secure fairer treatment of groups such as asylum seekers.

Downloadable evaluation report: http://westlondonalliance.org/

The guide *'What Works' in Community Cohesion* suggests that there are several factors behind successful myth busting work, including these:

- *Accessible language and format* – as in the Hull campaign, see below.
- *Using creative methods to reach groups that might not engage with normal media* – for example, young people.
- *Using interactive media, like radio phone-ins* – to give immediacy to the campaign and allow people to air their concerns.
- *Making good use of established forums* – such as residents' groups.
- *Incorporating 'myth busting' in other activities* – for example, work with young people might involve a debate about arranged marriages with views for and against.
- *Using a range of methods* – so that if one fails another might work.
- *Tailoring communication to local issues* – applying different approaches in different neighbourhoods, based on information about local concerns.
- *Reacting to national events* – for example, the Hull campaign (below) rapidly produced a leaflet responding to the 7/7 London bombings.

Hull's 'Don't Believe the Hype' campaign

This began with a leaflet published by the city council, in partnership with other agencies, including the police, the primary care trust (PCT) and Hull College. The leaflet uses a question and answer format to counter some common misconceptions about asylum seekers and the support they receive. It also sets out the positive contribution of immigrants to the UK economy. The leaflet was distributed via key community locations.

The leaflet has been complemented by other communications work, including radio phone-ins and local TV interviews by a member of the Refugee and Asylum Support Service. The 'Don't Believe the Hype' campaign is widely regarded by stakeholders as successful and is being rolled out to challenge myths around mental health.

Download the leaflet from: http://hullrefugeeweek.blogspot.com/

Working with communities

Earlier chapters in the guide covered the many aspects of work at community level and of engagement with tenants' and residents' groups. This final section looks at three issues which were covered in detail in the Commission's work: development work with Muslim communities, working with refugee and new migrant community organisations and promoting citizenship. Finally, it also looks at the way that community cohesion objectives relate to day-to-day work with tenants' and residents' groups.

Working with Muslim communities

The Commission makes the important point that, although the government is working with Muslim communities to prevent extremism, work to promote integration and cohesion is something different. Muslim communities have suffered from being associated with terror attacks and it is vital not to reinforce (perhaps accidentally) the impressions that people receive from the media that Muslim communities are hostile to or uninterested in integration. Muslim communities, and especially women and young people within the communities, can also be particularly isolated (often through poverty). Work to reduce such isolation is likely to require particular approaches and skills. Some of the factors to be borne in mind are:

- *Build on the experience of organisations already doing this work* – which are likely to be trusted by Muslim communities, and especially by women or young people within those communities.

- *Recognise the diversity of Muslim communities* – which may be long-standing communities, of third or fourth generations, or recently-arrived migrants (eg Somalis) or refugees (eg Iraqis).

- *Accept that Muslim communities may themselves not be cohesive* – there can be tensions between (for example) long-established communities and recently-arrived groups, or between different nationalities. Islam also (like Christianity) has profound divisions and people may be reluctant to bridge them.

- *Initial contact with communities may be with men* – so special effort, by female staff members, may be needed to engage with women, through separate consultation meetings.

- *Contacts with mosques can be important* – but young people (for example) may not be engaged religiously and contact may also need to be made through other channels (eg youth projects which bring together young people from different cultures).

- *Capacity building may be especially valuable in building confidence* – such as Ashram HA's work with Muslim women (see below).

- *Projects which bring ordinary people from different communities together are important* – chapter 4 discussed the need for 'bridging' between communities and this may be particularly important between Muslim and non-Muslim communities.

- *Evidence suggests that Muslim communities have similar priorities to everyone else* – housing opportunities, concern about crime, etc – and these can therefore be points of contact between communities.

Ashram HA has made particular efforts to engage with Muslim women, and one of its initiatives has helped to develop their skills and enable them to engage more readily with people from other communities.

Ashram's initiatives to engage Muslim women

More than half of Ashram's tenants are Muslim and so are one third of its staff. Ashram aims to reach out to Muslim women who may not have a strong community role, and to help them develop their capacities in a variety of ways – though sports, IT classes, design skills and business schemes. The aim is in part that they acquire new skills and increased self-confidence, but also that through these activities they become engaged with other communities. Several women who have taken part in Ashram's programmes report being less isolated than before and one Muslim woman has become an Ashram board member.

Source: Ashram HA *Engaging Muslim Communities*. Also see *Inside Housing*, 1st June 2007.

Working with Migrant and Refugee Community Organisations (MRCOs)

Many housing bodies are unfamiliar with the extent and range of community-based organisations which exist, formed by refugee or new migrant groups, and which have often sprung up in the last few years. Because of their recent development, these groups may not be engaged in the same networks as longer-established BME groups, may not be linked in with the local voluntary sector and may therefore be 'below the radar' when it comes to community engagement.

There are important reasons for starting to engage with MRCOs:

- they have important local knowledge about people's needs and experiences with coming to live in local neighbourhoods
- they provide the basis for engaging with people about how housing bodies can work with migrant/refugee communities to improve services
- they may already be offering services formally or informally and they may have potential to develop further
- government policy (in the refugee integration strategy *Integration Matters*) promotes the role of such local groups, as does the Housing Corporation in its guidance to HAs.

Many MRCOs serve particular national or ethnic groups (Somalis, Kurds, etc). Some cover broad geographical regions (Africa, Latin America), or are culturally-based (Arabic, Francophone). Yet others focus strongly on women's needs or deal with particular issues (children, disability, etc). MRCOs are found throughout Britain but are especially numerous in London and also in significant numbers in cities like Birmingham, Sheffield and Leicester.

Like any community-based groups, MRCOs represent a spectrum from newly-formed organisations (perhaps set up in response to new groups of migrants moving to a particular place, possibly because of asylum dispersal or because of work opportunities) to long-established bodies with a history of serving refugees or migrants over many years. Many groups have considerable demands made on them by asylum seekers, particularly those whose applications have been refused and who have limited or no resources.

The CIH guide to *Housing and Support Services for Asylum Seekers and Refugees* suggests that housing organisations might want to work with these community organisations in supporting the formation of emerging groups and in helping established groups develop their capacities. In terms of community cohesion, some of the ways in which involving MRCOs can be important are:

- *Knowledge of communities* – MRCOs may have, or may be able to provide, information about new communities which is not readily available to housing organisations (see the example on page 77).
- *A means of engagement about neighbourhood issues* – for example, to resolve the sort of low-level environmental issues that can be a source of conflict (see chapter 4).
- *A route for improving service delivery to marginalised groups* – either to get feedback on services, to work with the MRCO to make services more culturally-sensitive, or actually provide services (see example below).
- *A way of encouraging community-based social enterprises* – which can offer business opportunities to marginalised groups.

Haringey's Support for Small BME-led Service Providers[118]

Haringey's Supporting People team identified support needs among minority groups that they felt could best be met by community-based providers, who they would need to support if they were to deliver their contracts. The SP team therefore entered a Service Level Agreement with the council's Corporate Voluntary Sector Team (CVST) who now manage and monitor SP contracts with 12 small providers, including refugee organisations. The CVST's activities include:

- guidance for organisations to complete and submit SP documentation
- identifying funding opportunities for groups and assistance with bids
- promoting training opportunities and encouraging best practice
- identifying weaknesses within service provision and ensuring long-term sustainability of the organisation
- making and monitoring SP contract payments

→

---

118 Extracted from hact (forthcoming, 2008) *More Responsive Public Services? – A guide to commissioning migrant and refugee community organisations*. JRF.

- reconciling budgets; assessing audited accounts and annual reports
- maintenance of financial, administrative and monitoring systems.

The providers are contracted to support 302 people but the estimated number of people actually being supported is 719. In funding terms, £900,000 is invested in these services – 3.2% of the entire SP programme.

Further information: Stephanie.Rowland@haringey.gov.uk

The hact/CIH project *Opening Doors*, which is working with six HA partners to improve their services to refugees and migrants, has a specific focus on helping HAs engage with MRCOs. There are training materials available and there will be progress reports as the work develops (see Sources of Information at the end of the guide).

Promoting citizenship

Government policy puts considerable emphasis on encouraging people born abroad who have the right of permanent residence to become British citizens and satisfy the requirements about ability to speak English and knowledge of the UK (the 'Life in the UK' test). From a landlord perspective, promoting citizenship can be seen as an aid to integration at the individual level, and a way of helping people overcome the obstacles they may feel prevent them from participating (eg in residents' associations). Chapter 5 gave examples of social landlords helping tenants to improve their levels of English, and several now have links with colleges that provide ESOL courses. In Peterborough, housing agencies have combined with ESOL providers to create a wider citizenship programme.

Citizenship Programme For People In Peterborough

The 'Living in Peterborough, Life in the UK' programme is being run by the Peterborough ESOL Network (PEN) and funded by housing association Accent Nene, with Cross Keys Homes and the New Link Centre also supporting the programme.

The programme helps people with basic English skills to integrate further into the community. It teaches people how services, such as banks and shops, operate, and gives participants the opportunity to learn through hands-on experiences of visiting key local organisations around the city. Cultural background, local history and citizens' rights and responsibilities are also covered. At the end of the course participants can take a free ESOL or literacy exam.

The programme, compiled by PEN, is funded by Accent Nene through its 'Accent on Giving' fund, which was created to finance community projects.

→

Ghazala Bhatti, black and minority ethnic advisory officer for Cross Keys Homes, said: 'We already have some of our tenants looking to enrol on the course and would like to see even more join. We believe this is an excellent way of providing them with the necessary life and language skills to make a new and happy integrated life in Peterborough'.

The eight-week programmes are scheduled to continue over the next two years. For those eligible, the course is free of charge.

Further information: www.accentnene.org or www.crosskeyshomes.co.uk

Community cohesion principles and tenants' and residents' groups

Social landlords need to ensure that they become positive role models for inter-racial harmony in the neighbourhoods in which they work. In addition to the racial justice and business arguments for having employee and board profiles that reflect the ethnic composition of the areas the organisation serves, the visible presence in an area of multi-racial organisations that work well helps to reinforce positive messages.

Social landlords' responsibilities also extend to the way the organisation involves residents in decision making. From the community cohesion perspective, there are three main reasons why residents' involvement structures should mirror the extent of the diversity of residents living in social landlords' accommodation. First, structures that are ethnically unrepresentative may produce biased decision-making by the landlord. This can lead to inter-community resentment and hostility. Second, resident organisations are an important resource in promoting cohesion and tackling possible conflicts. Third, resident participation activities (committee meetings, working parties, social events) are themselves occasions where people meet and interact. They can therefore provide the context for inter-ethnic contact.

It is good practice for social landlords to set and monitor race equality and diversity targets for membership of tenants' and residents' associations, and to ensure that all parts of the community are able and encouraged to participate in them. There is detailed guidance on achieving this in *Encouraging Participation: A toolkit for tenants and social landlords*.[119] The Housing Diversity Network's website collects examples of good practice on working with residents on diversity issues – see below. The risks of assuming that minority ethnic groups find it easy to join resident participation

---

119 Millward, L *et al* (2003). CIH for JRF (see www.cih.org/publications/pub226.htm).

structures were highlighted in a study of Bradford, which found that there are often 'minorities within minorities' who do not participate, sometimes because of prejudice (for example, on caste lines) within their own communities.[120]

As we have emphasised through the examples in the guide, it is important to relate to people from different cultures, faiths, age groups and so on in a range of ways, reflecting the diversity of an area. However strong a residents' or tenants' group, there will always be people who do not take part and who might have to be reached in more inclusive and informal ways.

Housing Diversity Network Case Studies

Challenging Racism Guide for Tenants' & Residents' Associations in Kirklees

Kirklees Federation of Tenants' & Residents' Associations (KFTRA) have been active in developing their commitment and approach towards race equality and diversity. They have produced a practical guide for tenants associations on how to recognise, respond to and work towards overcoming racism.

Model Equal Opportunities Policy for Tenants' Associations

Many tenants' associations have a clause relating to equal opportunities within their constitution but working towards developing an equal opportunities policy can be a positive learning experience as well as a demonstration of commitment. KFTRA has developed a model equal opportunities policy for use by tenants' and residents' groups.

Embracing Diverse Communities: Helping to Promote Inclusion of Minority Ethnic Groups

Tenants, residents and their representative organisations have a central role to play in promoting equality, inclusion and community cohesion. The Race Equality for Tenants' Organisations Project has produced a best practice and training guide which could be used by tenants' groups themselves or by staff working with tenants' groups. It would also provide a starting point for developing policies and publicity material.

Further information: www.housingdiversitynetwork.co.uk

---

120 Blakey, H et al (2006) *Minorities within minorities: Beneath the surface of South Asian participation.* JRF.

Checklist on roles, responsibilities and partnerships

✓ Have housing organisations discussed the implications of the community cohesion agenda for their strategy and services?

✓ Have local authority strategy and enabling teams carried out a review of their role in the light of the community cohesion agenda?

✓ Are BME-led housing associations considering the community cohesion agenda and the diversification of their roles as part of their business planning?

✓ Does the organisation have a robust communications strategy about cohesion issues?

✓ And is it tackling local myths?

✓ Are local organisations based in minority ethnic communities drawn into decision-making and service provision?

✓ Does this include refugee and new migrant groups?

✓ Are community cohesion principles being followed by tenants' and residents' groups?

HOW COMMUNITY COHESION PRINCIPLES APPLY TO FUNDING OF COMMUNITY ORGANISATIONS

The Singh Commission (and the earlier Cantle report) questioned the principle of what the Commission calls 'single group funding' – that is, funding awarded 'on the basis of a particular identity, such as ethnic, religious or cultural'. The Commission called for a new approach to such funding and set out some recommended tests to be applied by local authorities and other funding bodies in future (see Annex D of the Commission's report).

This proposal has proved controversial, with representations against it being made by voluntary sector bodies. The government has not yet indicated whether policy will be changed along the lines recommended. Nevertheless, this section aims to provide guidance on this issue (but readers should check for any developments in government policy after publication).

The basis of 'single group funding'

On the face of it, favouring single groups would appear to be discrimination. But section 35 of the Race Relations Act allows 'positive action' which favours certain groups, provided it is justified.[121] The CRE code[122] gives examples of developing temporary accommodation especially for newly-arrived Somali refugees, sheltered housing for Chinese elders, providing wardens and carers who speak a particular Asian language, or meeting certain dietary and religious requirements. In these cases, to comply with the legislation, the housing organisation should have objective evidence of the need and ensure that its response is proportional. Unless it does so, it risks being challenged for unlawful discrimination.

The Singh Commission summarises the arguments it received for such single group funding as:

---

121 There is also a wider exemption that applies to certain charities, eg some charitable housing associations – see comments below.

122 CRE (2006), paras. 2.40-2.42.

- to meet needs not met by mainstream provision (especially those of newly-arrived people)
- because of a prior history of discrimination against these groups
- to provide culturally-sensitive services.

It also said that some funding is given on the basis of precedent – having given it in the past, it is difficult to refuse it in similar circumstances now.

It is worth making a distinction (not made in the Commission's report) between the organisation receiving the funding, and the service provided. For example, if a registered BME housing association receives funding, it should be regarded as single group funding *only* if it is for a 'positive action' project of the kind described. The fact that it is a BME-led body receiving it is not (in itself) relevant. For example, the kind of development described in chapter 5, intended to expand housing opportunities for BME communities, is not single group funding because such developments are invariably open to all communities, it is simply that marketing of them prioritises certain communities.

The issues for community cohesion

If a project or service is aimed exclusively at certain groups it poses a dilemma for community cohesion in several ways. First, it immediately raises the issue of why that group should get a special service (and funding) not available to others? This may be particularly the case with funding for major schemes, such as a sheltered housing scheme, in areas with considerable housing demand. Second, a service offered in an exclusive way (eg solely in a minority language) could be argued to discourage integration by promoting dependency, rather than encouraging people to make use of generally-available services. Third, if a project reinforces the 'distinct identity' of a community (eg in cultural or religious terms), does that also reinforce its differences with other communities?

There are also community cohesion arguments *in favour of* services aimed at certain groups. For example, if a particular group has acute needs which are not being met, or if new migrant communities require targeted help in order to aid their integration.

In addition, some kinds of project may only offer a short-term service (eg a hostel for Asian women fleeing domestic violence) and their effect on community cohesion may therefore be minimal.

These are real dilemmas which housing organisations, as both funding bodies and service providers, have to address on a case-by-case basis.

The Singh Commission proposals

The Commission says that there should be a presumption against single group funding unless there is a clear need for capacity building within a group or community. It says that, if single group funding is nevertheless awarded:

- reasons should be publicised to all communities in the local area
- before receiving further funding, the group should demonstrate how it is becoming more 'outward facing' and starting to follow integration and cohesion principles.

The Commission also recommends government to:

- produce guidelines about single group funding that reflect integration and cohesion principles
- ensure that mainstream service providers 'improve their offer' to particular communities so that single group funding is no longer felt necessary.

The implications for housing organisations

This issue affects housing organisations in a number of potential ways:

- In their strategic roles, for example, planning for new housing provision or reviewing strategies for housing-related support under Supporting People.
- As enabling bodies which might make grants to, or commission services from, community-based organisations.
- As direct service providers, planning or delivering services aimed at addressing particular needs.

This guide includes recommendations and practical examples about cases where single group funding has been used specifically to promote cohesion – for example, encouraging Muslim women to be less isolated (page 157) or capacity building among Somali people to allow them to survey and report on their community's needs (page 77). In these examples, evidence could show that the groups currently participate less than others, and there was a clear community cohesion case for using resources to enable them to become more engaged in their areas and with mainstream services.

Services to meet particular needs

The arguments are less clear cut in cases where funding is not to promote engagement but for services to meet new or unmet needs, or provide otherwise unavailable culturally-sensitive services. The key tests here are:

1. If the service is to meet needs for people who cannot yet be expected to access mainstream services easily (eg a new migrant community), does it include an element which will help them to access mainstream services in the future (rather than encourage continued dependency on the special service)?

2. If the need is for a culturally-sensitive service, can the need be specified clearly and the additional requirements compared with a mainstream service made clear?

3. Can such a service be delivered in a way that promotes integration, for example by offering the service more widely and in English as well as in a minority language? Or by promoting contact (eg between Asian elders in a sheltered scheme and other communities)? Or by ensuring a service for new migrants caters for a range of groups (as migration patterns change)?

4. Can the project or service be used to influence mainstream provision or facilitate access to it, for example by helping people with paperwork or by showing mainstream providers what the gaps are in their services?

5. Is the organisation providing the service engaged with other communities and can it show how its services contribute to community cohesion more widely?

Although the Race Relations Act does provide exemption for certain charities (that enables them to favour a particular racial group over another), careful consideration needs to be given to the potential impact on cohesion and integration, even when the service provided clearly complies with the law.

Even if the tests set out above cannot be satisfied immediately, there may be a pressing need for a service which should nevertheless be met. In all cases, the Commission's recommendations about transparency and explaining the reasons for decisions should be followed, and the opportunities for a greater community cohesion element in the service pursued at a later date (eg as the Commission says – before funding is renewed).

Checklist on single group funding

✓ Is there a demonstrated case for a separate service or project outside mainstream provision?

✓ Can the service be delivered in a way that is not exclusive?

✓ How will it help people access mainstream services, or encourage mainstream providers to fill gaps in services?

✓ What measures are being taken to encourage integration and community cohesion by the organisation providing the service?

✓ Can the service being funded itself contribute towards integration/cohesion?

✓ Has there been a transparent process for making decisions on funding, including consultation with other local community organisations?

✓ Will there be monitoring of the impact of the service and how it leads to greater integration/cohesion?

✓ How will the funding be publicised and justified?

APPENDIX 2

HOW COMMUNITY COHESION PRINCIPLES APPLY TO TRANSLATION AND TO INTERPRETER SERVICES

The Singh Commission places considerable emphasis on people being able to speak English, as a prerequisite for successful integration. Speaking English is obviously key to interaction between people, assisting in breaking down prejudice, helping people into training or employment and hence reducing inequalities.

The Commission therefore questions whether the widespread practice of translating information about services into a range of community languages should continue, and sets out guidelines which it believes should be followed. Its assessment and the guidelines apply to translation of generally-available material, although it says that some principles may apply too in cases where interpreters are used or one-off translations made.

Typically translations are used to:

- ensure people can access essential services
- give access to the democratic process, eg take part in meetings
- support new migrant groups or groups who don't speak English
- allow people to understand local rules, eg parking restrictions
- comply with race relations requirements not to discriminate against people in their access to services.

The Commission issues a reminder that there is no legal reason for all materials to be translated, and that the main barrier people face is inability to speak English. Community cohesion principles should apply to decisions about when and what to translate – and communication with and between all groups should be considered.

The Commission suggests a set of questions to be asked when considering translation, which can be summarised as:

- Is it essential to translate it?
- Should it be translated in full?

- Are the languages chosen appropriate and do they reflect the communities at which the material is aimed?
- Is it value for money?
- Do other agencies have the materials available already?
- As well as producing the translation, can you support people in the community to learn English?
- Are you keeping up-to-date with changes in the community that affect the need for translations?
- Do you have a communication strategy applying to all residents, which includes criteria on when to translate?

On the basis of these guidelines, housing organisations are recommended to:

1. Build up a picture of the communication requirements of residents – can they speak English / read English? Do they have disabilities – visual, hearing or learning disabilities – that require special measures?

2. Where minority language needs are identified, find out if people are literate in their mother tongue? – or should translation be verbal?

3. Respond to demand rather than automatically translating literature – use a logo which says (in relevant languages) 'we would be happy to explain or translate this leaflet for you'.

4. Identify residents' needs and willingness to learn English and work with local partners (including community organisations) to support these skills.

5. Monitor use of translation or interpretation services at the same time as clearly communicating opportunities to learn English, to judge their value over time.

6. Consider the value for money of different approaches, eg language courses versus providing interpreter services.

7. Be aware of when it is not realistic or practical to provide translations (eg translated documents do not have legal status in the UK – so this prevents translated tenancy agreements from having legal standing – but it may mean that extra effort is needed to explain them).

8. Have a system for ensuring that letters, leaflets, etc are written in plain English, avoiding jargon (or when it is really needed, explaining it properly).

9. Where translations are used, design literature so that English is on one page with the translated material on the facing page.

10. Train staff how to speak to customers in a jargon-free way that makes their messages clear to all users of the service.

Sources of Information

Reports and guides referred to in the text

Audit Commission (2007) *Crossing Borders – Responding to the local challenges of migrant workers.*

Bailey, N et al (2006) *Creating and Sustaining Mixed Income Communities: A good practice guide.* CIH for JRF.

Blackaby, B and Chahal, K (2000) *Black and Minority Ethnic Housing Strategies.* CIH and Federation of Black Housing Associations.

Blakey, H et al (2006) *Minorities within minorities: Beneath the surface of South Asian participation.* JRF.

Campbell Tickell (2005) *BME Housing Associations and Stock Transfers.* Housing Corporation.

Centre for Urban and Regional Studies (2004) *Empowering communities, improving housing: Involving black and minority ethnic tenants and communities.* CLG.

CIH (2003) *Providing a Safe Haven: Housing Asylum Seekers and Refugees.*

Coles, B, England, J, and Rugg, J (1998) *Working with Young People on Estates: The Role of Housing Professionals in Multi-Agency Work.* CIH for JRF.

Commission for Racial Equality (2006) *Code of Practice on Race Equality in Housing.*

Commission on Integration and Cohesion (2007) *Our Shared Future.* CLG.

Commission on Integration and Cohesion (2007) *Integration and Cohesion Case Studies.* CLG.

CLG (2006) *Respect and Housing Management – Using good neighbour agreements.*

CLG (2006) *Strong and Prosperous Communities: The Local Government White Paper.*

CLG (2007) *A Framework for Fairness: Proposals for a Single Equality Bill for Great Britain.*

CLG (2007) *'What Works' in Community Cohesion: Research study for the Commission on Integration and Cohesion.*

CLG (2007) *Improving Opportunity, Strengthening Society: Two years on. A progress report on the government's strategy for race equality and community cohesion.*

Dearling, A, Newburn, T and Somerville, P (2006) *Supporting Safer Communities: Housing, crime and neighbourhoods.* CIH.

Department of the Environment, Transport and the Regions, Housing Corporation and National Assembly for Wales (2001) *Tackling Racial Harassment: Code of Practice for Social Landlords.*

Duncan, P and Thomas, S (2007) *Successful Neighbourhoods: A good practice guide.* CIH.

Fitzpatrick, S (2004) *Poverty of Place* (available from www.pm.gov.uk/output/Page10025.asp).

Folkard, K (1998) *Housing Strategies for Youth: A good practice guide.* CIH and Local Government Association.

Fotheringham, D and Perry, J (2003) *Offering Communities Real Choice: Lettings and Community Cohesion.* CIH.

Groves, R, Middleton, A, Murie, A and Broughton, K (2003) *Neighbourhoods that Work: A Study of the Bournville Estate, Birmingham.* The Policy Press.

HACAS Chapman Hendy (2003) *Empowering Communities: The Community Gateway Model.* CIH.

Hact (forthcoming 2008) *More Responsive Public Services? – A guide to commissioning migrant and refugee community organisations.* JRF.

Harrison, M and Phillips, D (2003) *Housing and Black and Minority Ethnic Communities: Review of the Evidence Base.* Office of Deputy Prime Minister.

Harrison, M, Phillips, D, Chahal, K, Hunt, L and Perry, J (2005) *Housing, 'Race' and Community Cohesion.* CIH.

Hawtin, M, Kettle, J, Moran, C and Crossley, R (1999) *Housing Integration and Resident Participation: Evaluation of a project to help integrate black and minority ethnic tenants.* York Publishing Services for JRF.

Hills, J (2007) *Ends and Means – The future roles of social housing in England.* Centre for Analysis of Social Exclusion, London School of Economics.

Holmes, C (2006) *Mixed Communities: Success and Sustainability.* JRF 'Foundations'.

Homeless Link (2006) *A8 Nationals in London Homelessness Services.*

Home Office (2001) *Community Cohesion: Report of the Independent Review Team Chaired by Ted Cantle.*

Home Office (2003) *Building a Picture of Community Cohesion: A Guide for Local Authorities and their Partners.* Home Office, LGA, Commission for Racial Equality, Office of the Deputy Prime Minister and Neighbourhood Renewal Unit.

Home Office (2004) *Firm Foundations: The Government's Framework for Community Capacity Building.*

Home Office and Office of the Deputy Prime Minister (2004) *Building Community Cohesion into Area-Based Initiatives.*

Home Office and Office of the Deputy Prime Minister (2005) *Community Cohesion: Seven Steps - A practitioner's toolkit.*

Home Office (2005) *Integration Matters: A national strategy for refugee integration.*

Housing Corporation (2002) *The Way Forward: Our Approach to Regulation.*

Housing Corporation (2002) *Regulatory Code Good Practice Note: Race Equality and Diversity.*

IDeA/LGA (2006) *Leading Cohesive Communities: A guide for local authority leaders and chief executives.* LGA (with IDeA, Home Office, Office of the Deputy Prime Minister and Audit Commission).

IDeA (2007) *New European Migration: Good practice guide for local authorities.*

Institute for Community Cohesion (2007) *A Practical Guide to Tension Monitoring for Local Authorities, Police Services and Partner Agencies.*

Leask, P (2004) *Bringing Communities Closer: A report on the work of the West London Community Cohesion Pathfinder.*

Lemos, G (2004) *Community Conflict: Causes and Action.* Lemos and Crane.

Lemos, G (2005) *The Search for Tolerance – Challenging and changing racist attitudes among young people.* JRF.

Lister, S, Perry, J and Thornley, M (2007) *Community Engagement in Housing-Led Regeneration: A good practice guide.* CIH.

Local Government Association (2002) *Guidance on Community Cohesion.* LGA, Office of the Deputy Prime Minister, Home Office, Commission for Racial Equality and Interfaith Network for the United Kingdom.

Local Government Association (2004) *Community Cohesion: An action guide.* LGA (with the Home Office, ODPM, CRE, IDeA).

Lupton, M and Perry, J (2004) *The Future of Black and Minority Ethnic Housing Associations.* CIH and Housing Corporation.

Millward, I, Beckford, J, Dougal, A and Reid, B (2003) *Encouraging Participation: A Toolkit for Tenants and Social Landlords.* CIH for JRF.

Muir, R (2007) *One London? – Change and cohesion in three London boroughs.* IPPR.

Nixon, J and Hunter, C (2006) *Tackling Anti-Social Behaviour: Action Frameworks.* CIH for JRF.

Office of the Deputy Prime Minister (2003) *Sustainable Communities: Building for the Future.*

Oldfield King Planning Ltd (1998) *Accommodating Diversity: Housing design in a multicultural society.* National Housing Federation.

Pawson, H et al (2006) *Monitoring the Longer-Term Impact of Choice-Based Lettings.* CLG.

Perry, J (2005) *Housing and Support Services for Asylum Seekers and Refugees.* CIH for JRF.

Platt, L (2007) *Poverty and Ethnicity in the UK.* JRF.

Ratcliffe, P et al (1996) *'Race' and Housing in Bradford: Addressing the Needs of South Asian, African and Caribbean Communities.* Bradford Housing Forum.

Ratcliffe, P et al (2001) *Breaking Down the Barriers: Improving Asian Access to Social Rented Housing.* CIH.

Refugee Housing Association (2005) *Reducing Barriers for Refugees Accessing Choice-Based Lettings Schemes.*

Richardson, J (2007) *Providing Gypsy and Traveller sites: Contentious spaces.* CIH for JRF.

Robinson, D et al (2004) *How Housing Management can Contribute to Community Cohesion.* CIH.

Robinson, D and Reeve, K (2006) *Neighbourhood Experiences of New Migration.* York Publishing Services for JRF.

Silverman, E et al (2005) *A Good Place for Children? - Attracting and Retaining Families in inner urban mixed income communities.* CIH for JRF.

Social Exclusion Unit (2001) *A New Commitment to Neighbourhood Renewal: National Strategy Action Plan.*

Spencer, S et al (2007) *Migrants' Lives Beyond the Workplace – the experiences of Central and East Europeans in the UK.* JRF.

Sustainable Development Commission (2004) *Sustainable Communities and Sustainable Development – A review of the Sustainable Communities Plan* (available at http://www.sd-commission.org.uk/index.php).

Vertovec, S (2007) *New complexities of cohesion in Britain: Superdiversity, transnationalism and civil integration.*

Wadhams, C (2006) *An Opportunity Waiting to Happen: Housing associations as 'community anchors'.* Hact/NHF.

Websites with further information
Many of the publications above can be downloaded or purchased from the following websites.

Audit Commission
www.audit-commission.gov.uk

Chartered Institute of Housing
www.cih.org

Commission for Equality and Human Rights
www.cehr.org.uk/

Commission for Racial Equality (until October 2007)
www.cre.gov.uk

Commission on Integration and Cohesion
www.integrationandcohesion.org.uk

Communities and Local Government
www.communities.gov.uk

Housing Associations' Charitable Trust (hact)
www.hact.org.uk

Home Office
www.homeoffice.gov.uk

Housing Corporation
www.housingcorp.gov.uk

Improvement and Development Agency for Local Government (IDeA)
www.idea.gov.uk

Institute for Community Cohesion
www.coventry.ac.uk/icoco/a/264

Joseph Rowntree Foundation
www.jrf.org.uk

Local Government Association
www.lga.gov.uk

Neighbourhood Renewal Unit
www.neighbourhood.gov.uk/

Web-based resources referred to in the guide
Opening Doors (joint hact/CIH project funded by the Housing Corporation and CLG):
www.cih.org/policy/openingdoors/

New European Migration toolkit:
www.idea.gov.uk/idk/core/page.do?pageId=6949778

Web resources on new migration based on the Audit Commission report *Crossing Borders* (including guidance on data sources, local case studies, etc):
www.audit-commission.gov.uk/migrantworkers/

In addition, the CohesionActionNet, RaceActionNet and RenewalNet websites have practical examples of cohesion work, and the ICAR website has well-presented and detailed information on asylum and refugee issues:
   www.cohesionactionnet.org.uk/
   www.raceactionnet.co.uk
   www.renewal.net/
   www.icar.org.uk

Other titles from CIH

The Chartered Institute of Housing has a range of publications relevant to communities and neighbourhoods. Here are details of two recent Good Practice Guides.

For details of all CIH publications, and information on postage and packing charges and discounts for CIH members and students, contact CIH publications:
Tel: 024 7685 1700   E-mail: pubs@cih.org   Website: www.cih.org/services/publications

Successful Neighbourhoods
A Good Practice Guide

Pete Duncan and Sally Thomas

Housing providers are part of an emerging political and professional consensus about focusing on neighbourhoods and increasing the involvement and influence of the people who live and work there. This new good practice guide equips readers with an understanding of the fast-moving neighbourhood agenda and makes a strong case for housing organisations to play an active role in supporting the neighbourhoods where they are key stakeholders.

Packed with inspiring examples from a wide range of areas, the guide celebrates the transformation already achieved in some neighbourhoods, while challenging many more housing organisations to make this success widespread. With particular emphasis on neighbourhood management as a way of achieving lasting change, the guide provides practical guidance on the closely-related issues of improving local services and empowering local communities.

The guide includes information on how to:
- Identify and implement ways to shift from managing housing stock to managing places
- Develop and sustain effective partnerships
- Build capacity in communities and organisations
- Evaluate impacts and outcomes.

The guide is aimed at housing professionals and other people who are directly involved in managing and renewing neighbourhoods. It should also be of interest to a broad range of policy-makers, community stakeholders and people active in their own communities.

The authors are co-directors of Social Regeneration Consultants and specialise in community-based urban regeneration. They have considerable hands-on experience of neighbourhood-based programmes and previously wrote CIH's 2001 Good Practice Guide on Neighbourhood Management.

ISBN 978 1 905018 28 4
CIH members £22.50   Non-members £28.00

Community Engagement in Housing-Led Regeneration
A Good Practice Guide

Sam Lister, John Perry and Marilyn Thornley

Regeneration can only be effective if it successfully engages with the communities it affects. This is a lesson learned and applied in the nine Housing Market Renewal Pathfinders in the North and the Midlands. Their experiences, and the new methods they have developed and tested, are relevant to all housing-led regeneration initiatives which depend on community engagement.

The guide addresses the question 'why engage with communities' and part II then looks in detail at what engagement means at strategic level, at neighbourhood level, and in decision-making on individual streets and houses. It has more than fifty practical examples from the Pathfinders and other regeneration schemes. It considers methods of engagement in detail, including those needed to involve 'hard-to-reach' groups including young people, older people and newcomers to communities (such as asylum seekers).

Detailed chapters in part III of the guide address particular issues:
- Skills needed for community engagement
- Using consultants
- Community cohesion and regeneration
- The town planning system
- Community capacity building
- Dealing with the media.

An annex provides recommended CIH/TPAS standards for community engagement, which can be adapted to local circumstances.

This guide is the only one available that is relevant to housing-led regeneration and it is essential reading for all those involved in regenerating older or poorer neighbourhoods.

ISBN 978 1 905018 52 9
CIH members £22.50   Non-members £28.00